The
Dojo Coach's
Pocket Guide

The Dojo Coach's Pocket Guide

Maximizing Immersive Learning *for* Agile Teams

Jess Brock

BK
Berrett–Koehler Publishers, Inc.

Berrett-Koehler Publishers, Inc.
1333 Broadway, Suite 1000
Oakland, CA 94612-1921
Tel: (510) 817-2277
Fax: (510) 817-2278
www.bkconnection.com

ORDERING INFORMATION
Quantity sales. Special discounts are available on quantity purchases by corporations, associations, and others. For details, contact the "Special Sales Department" at the Berrett-Koehler address above.
Individual sales. Berrett-Koehler publications are available through most bookstores. They can also be ordered directly from Berrett-Koehler:
Tel: (800) 929-2929; Fax: (802) 864-7626; www.bkconnection.com.
Orders for college textbook / course adoption use.
Please contact Berrett-Koehler: Tel: (800) 929-2929; Fax: (802) 864-7626.

Distributed to the U.S. trade and internationally by Penguin Random House Publisher Services.

Berrett-Koehler and the BK logo are registered trademarks of Berrett-Koehler Publishers, Inc.

Printed in the United States of America

Berrett-Koehler books are printed on long-lasting acid-free paper. When it is available, we choose paper that has been manufactured by environmentally responsible processes. These may include using trees grown in sustainable forests, incorporating recycled paper, minimizing chlorine in bleaching, or recycling the energy produced at the paper mill.

Library of Congress Cataloging-in-Publication Data

Names: Brock, Jess, author.
Title: The dojo coach's pocket guide : maximizing immersive learning for agile teams / Jess Brock.
Description: First edition. | Oakland, CA : Berrett-Koehler Publishers, Inc., [2023] | Includes index.
Identifiers: LCCN 2022056115 (print) | LCCN 2022056116 (ebook) | ISBN 9781523002726 (paperback) | ISBN 9781523002733 (pdf) | ISBN 9781523002740 (epub) | ISBN 9781523002757 (audio)
Subjects: LCSH: Software engineering—Management. | Computer software—Development. | Employees—Coaching of. | Teams in the workplace—Management.
Classification: LCC QA76.758 .B748 2023 (print) | LCC QA76.758 (ebook) | DDC 005.1068—dc23/eng/20230313
LC record available at https://lccn.loc.gov/2022056115
LC ebook record available at https://lccn.loc.gov/2022056116

First Edition
31 30 29 28 27 26 25 24 23   10 9 8 7 6 5 4 3 2 1

Book production: Westchester Publishing Services
Cover design: Debbie Berne

For my wife, Emily, for putting up with my harebrained ideas, crude humor, and devilish good looks. I love you a lot, a lot.

For my daughter, Suren, for unknowingly motivating me to be the best version of myself. To say that I owe you my life would be an understatement. I love you, Dip.

Contents

Who Is This Book Meant For?

This book is meant for Dojo coaches in the Agile, product, DevOps, and software development space—specifically, two audiences:

- fledgling Dojo coaches who seek to enhance their capabilities (for example, Agile coaches or technical coaches)
- experienced Dojo coaches who seek to enhance their capabilities

What to Expect from This Book

It is important to understand that to get the most from this book, you should have a base-level understanding of immersive learning Dojos as they relate to Agile teams. This book will not provide education on the foundational concepts or theories of the Dojo. Instead, it is meant to provide tactical advice to Dojo coaches on ways to maximize the effectiveness of their Dojo.

Fortunately, there are resources that provide the core whats and whys of immersive learning Dojos. I would've regretted not having them as I started my Dojo coaching journey. They include the following:

- *Creating Your Dojo: Upskill Your Organization for Digital Evolution*, by Dion Stewart and Joel Tosi—This book is an essential read for anyone new to Dojos because it defines the timeless Dojo Roadmap. I strongly encourage you to Google Dion and Joel, as anything they contribute to the Dojo community is pure gold. I have immense respect for these folks because they helped inspire my coaching and the book you're reading right now. Specifically, I strongly recommend that you familiarize yourself with the section called "Isn't Dojo coaching essentially coaching but timeboxed?" in the FAQs at the end of the book. Having an understanding of this content will help you to draw value from this book.

- Dojo Consortium (dojoconsortium.org)—This is where practicing Dojo coaches go to meld minds and grow Dojo best practices for the greater good.
- Target Dojo (dojo.target.com)—Major retailer Target helped pioneer immersive learning Dojos. Its Dojo is considered a leader in the space, and rightfully so. Target's Dojo coaches have contributed to the broader Dojo community in so many ways that I've lost count. You are sure to learn a thing or two by paying their website a visit and by exploring the web for Target Dojo goodies.

A Note about Dojo Roles

Some publications distinguish between Dojo staff (e.g., administrators) and Dojo coaches (or Agile coaches, product coaches, and technical coaches). For the purposes of this book, I exclusively use *Dojo coach* to refer to a blanket role that could mean any of those roles. If you are lucky enough to be staffed with each of these individual roles, that is a terrific position to be in. But I do not see that level of Dojo staffing often and therefore wanted to cater to something that resembled reality over greenfields.

Cultural Respect: Honoring, Not Borrowing

Because Dojos are a respected fixture in Japanese culture, we must remain sensitive about the issue of cultural appropriation. I am not of Japanese descent or a practitioner of Japanese martial arts and therefore cannot and will not represent traditional Dojos. Hence, it is my ethical responsibility to remind us to be keen on nurturing cultural appreciation and eliminate any risk of cultural appropriation.

The best way to remain culturally sensitive is to stay persistent on acknowledgment, engage in compassionate dialogue, respect boundaries, and pursue the Dojo concept with the highest level of regard and appreciation.

In other words, it is not enough to just talk about it; we must follow through with action.

Introduction

THE BOOK'S DEFINITION OF "DOJO"

Do·jo: A six-week immersive learning engagement that embodies the "learn by doing" approach, whereby learning and delivery occur simultaneously. Areas of focus: Agile, product, DevOps, and software development.

All Dojo coaches have a big thing in common. Nope, it is not a fondness for crippling dad jokes or high caffeine consumption. Good guesses, though.

They intend to intersect learning with delivery as an outcome of coaching teams.

The commonality is the crucial difference between a Dojo coach and other types of coaches. And what a fantastic differentiator it is! As a Dojo coach, you are encouraged to respond to the learning and delivery needs of the team. No prescriptions. No agendas. You do what you need to do to grow that person or team. That means if a critical bug was detected in production during the Dojo, you could shift the team to a whole-team mob to get it fixed. While that scenario seems squirrely and counter to learning, Dojo coaches know that fire drills are the best learning opportunities. Not only did the team fix the bug, but they've also fixed it faster than they usually would. They've adhered to their quality standards, built up their mobbing capabilities, and exposed some team members to a part of the codebase that was unfamiliar to them. How cool is that?

Immersive learning Dojos support healthy learning retention. I've checked on teams months after the Dojo concluded, and they are still using what they learned; in some cases, they are even building off what they've learned and now teaching us new things. When I try to rationalize the unheard-of retention, I go back to the essence of Dojos: that the team practices what they learned immediately using the work in their backlog and remaining within their unique context. Does this sense of "home" have some magical power over neural pathway development? I am not sure about the smart brain stuff, but I am sure that Dojos have been transformative for team growth.

Although, as transformative as Dojos can be, it can be considered shocking or impressive, depending on how you look at it, that a fair number of Dojo coaches have winged it so far. Being in that camp myself, I have learned *a lot* through trial and error in the Dojo. I would have greatly appreciated more detailed, practical guidance for sheer pain avoidance and confidence building.

Mistakes, inefficiencies, and flops need not be repeated to become a formidable Dojo coach, and that is precisely why I wrote this book.

I've leveraged my experience as a Dojo coach. I have collated other Dojo coaches' experiences to bring you this no-nonsense pocket guide straight from the field of immersive learning Dojos—across various sectors, organizations, and constraints.

Not sure which team to select when you're assessing candidate teams? Consult this pocket guide. Need to know how to sell the Dojo to your leadership? It's covered in the pocket guide. Need a gut check to ensure that you're not exhibiting Dojo coach antipatterns? Pocket guide.

Dojo coaches: this pocket guide is your new companion. It sheds light on the unfamiliar territory to give you confidence, offering actionable and powerful advice so you can get things done right and providing much-needed support as you navigate the worthwhile journey of developing people.

Does this book provide all of the answers to Dojo coaching? No. But could it help you improve your Dojo in some way? Yes. Could it inspire Dojo coaches to challenge current Dojo coaching practices and incite collaboration toward making the Dojo that we know and love better than ever? Gosh, I hope so!

All right, that's enough introduction.

Are you ready to ramp up your Dojo coaching game? We're going to get right into the details. Don't pretend I didn't warn you!

Supporting materials for this book can be found at
dojopocketguide.com

---

1 ■ Dojo Coaching Principles

In matters of style, swim with the current; in matters of principle,
stand like a rock.

—Thomas Jefferson

According to *Merriam-Webster's*, a principle is a general or basic truth
on which other truths or theories can be based. So it makes good
sense to start this book with the Dojo coaching principles. In this
way, we are entering Dojo coaching at its foundation, where the rest
of the content will build from.

The undeniable truth is that out in the field you will run into all
kinds of constraints, situational complexities, and politics. They usually present as challenges, but if you manage to navigate them and nail
your goals, it feels really damn good. While the fundamental ethos
of coaching is to lead with empathy and be adaptable to the needs of
the coachee (shaping your coaching to accommodate their complexities, constraints, and politics), there is value in nonnegotiables to

maintain coaching integrity. I like to think of principles as the light-house that guides us when we're lost at sea. You may explore the ocean, but if you get lost you can be guided back home.

Dojo Principle #1: Six-Week Minimum

On initial glance, six weeks of full dedication for one team does not sell well. Why? Because it comes across as expensive or excessive.

In my experience selling the Dojo as a consultant and as a full-time employee, the Dojo looks like a $25,000–$50,000 statement of work for a single team and presents as a $120,000–$200,000 salary for a coach who can feasibly coach just four to five Agile teams or about 45 people in a calendar year. The Dojo model doesn't appear to scale well, and leadership naturally raises an eyebrow when being approached with a large monetary ask and seemingly small impact.

In order to make the Dojo appear more cost effective, one might reduce the six-week length so they may fit more Dojos in for the same amount of time and cost. As tempting as this seems, *don't do it*. You may as well not pursue a Dojo if you reduce the length to anything less than six weeks.

I will beat this point to death throughout this book, but the summarized reason for keeping to at least six weeks is that anything less does not allow a team enough time to get in adequate practice and repetition. Repetition is key because it helps transition a skill from the conscious to the subconscious. The conscious-to-subconscious shift can take the form of developing muscle memory or unlearning bad habits.

There is an entire chapter called "Making the Case for the Dojo" that delves into how to sell the Dojo so that leadership can see the long-term investment that helps them overcome the initial sticker shock.

Dojo Principle #2: Learning Is Greater Than Delivery

The Dojo's greatest benefit is that it develops skills while delivering real work. This unique intersection of learning and delivery is powerful because doing the real thing has been proved to be more retentive than other forms of learning. We'll explore why that is when we cover Edgar Dale's Cone of Experience later in the book.

Here's the thing: in the real world learning and delivery are often at odds. Companies acknowledge that they need to develop their people but simultaneously feel pressure to deliver business outcomes. In most cases, delivery reigns supreme and learning is deprioritized.

Keeping to the scope of the book, what if delivery starts distracting a team from the intended learning of a Dojo? Quick answer: eliminate the learning distraction or stop the Dojo altogether. This sounds harsh, but we don't call it a principle for nothing.

As part of the initial conversations with leadership and the Dojo candidate teams, we set the clear expectation that learning is the priority of the Dojo. Leaders should ensure that the team is able to focus on learning for the full six weeks, whether that means providing extra air cover or setting expectations with stakeholders. We'll get into the specifics of what these conversations should look like in Chapter 2.

The expected approach of a Dojo is to "slow down to speed up." Delivery will remain continuous, but there will likely be dips in velocity in the first few weeks of the engagement as the team acclimates to everything that comes with the Dojo—Dojo coaches, new skills and practices, experimentation, and so on.

The intent of the Dojo is that the team's new normal is an improved status quo, but the only surefire way to ensure that this happens is to ensure that learning remains on top.

Dojo Principle #3: Optimal Team Profile (Ready, Willing, and Available)

Ready, willing, and available belong together as one principle because they are interconnected as the desired profile of a Dojo team.

We'll break them down one by one:

- Ready: The team is filled with energy and ready to get after it.

- Willing: The team is willing to do whatever it takes to maximize their time in the Dojo.
- Available: The team is logistically available and free from near-term deadlines or a significant amount of out-of-office.

I have had Dojo opportunities seem appealing on the surface; the work was exciting, the leadership had bought in, calendars miraculously lined up. But when we got to talking to the team, it was clear they were not ready, willing, and available. This situation is bound to happen. It could be caused by a number of things—it could be something straightforward like they have a bunch of out-of-office coming up, or it could be something more serious like the team doesn't have faith in leadership's ability to support their learning.

No matter the case, the best thing to do is to hold off on pursuing a Dojo with the team and establish a check-in cadence with them so the relationship is maintained. Some of the best Dojos I've participated in were with teams that started with "not now, but later." Perhaps it was the absence of imposition that helped the teams connect better with the Dojo coaches.

Dojo Principle #4: Maximize Your Time

The honest truth is that, as a Dojo coach, you have a finite timebox of six weeks to make a long-term impact on people in deep areas such as skill sets, mindsets, and work life. That is a lot to do in a small amount of time! I struggle to find the words to convey how fast the six weeks fly by.

When you are in the business of Dojo coaching, making every single day count is your default mode. This means being planful about how to approach Dojo goals and relationship building (examining day by day, week by week). It also means navigating on the fly, such as by pivoting if a learning approach isn't working.

In order to stay plugged in to determine the best use of time, you will depend on frequent communication with fellow Dojo coaches and the Dojo team. Often, it is a daily collaboration to ensure everyone is aligned and the given day has been seized to the best of the group's abilities.

If distractions hinder your ability to maximize coaching impact in the Dojo, you must address them immediately. Before you know it, it is week 5 and your Dojo goals are nowhere near target, and that doesn't help the reputation of the Dojo and it most certainly does not help the team's learning journey. We've got six weeks to affect lives, and the word *urgency* truly is not strong enough.

We'll get into more time-maximization techniques later in the book, but for the purposes of introducing this principle, the message should be clear: let's move, people!

Don't Budge

Consider the four Dojo coaching principles—six-week minimum, learning over delivery, optimal team profile, and time maximization—as worthy reasons to "die on the hill" because they are fundamental to a successful Dojo. Your unique adaptations and coaching styles are encouraged, but do not budge on the principles.

Now that we have a foundation established, let's move to the practical side of Dojo coaching.

2 ■ Navigating the Dojo Roadmap

Every team is different. They have their own constraints, their own strengths, their own challenges, and their own mix of people and personalities. So it's safe to assume that every Dojo engagement is different, too.

A defined flow for facilitating the Dojo becomes integral for operational efficiency and headache reduction, and it helps to keep focus and alignment amid the variance and unpredictability.

With a well-defined plan, we can grow the Dojo product with a consistent methodology. Esteemed author Jonathan Smart has said, "Nail it before you scale it," implying that making changes to procedures is easier when fewer participants are depending on those procedures.

All said, I have decided to present the broader Dojo flow (from start to finish) in a roadmap form. The Dojo Roadmap, as I've called it (originality points!), is a win for efficiency and effectiveness because it prevents Dojo coaches from reinventing the wheel and it builds confidence because it makes Dojo coaches surefooted on the path for achieving outcomes.

The Dojo Roadmap is open to adaptation and is definitely not meant to be a prescription. Its primary intent is to reduce the administrative overhead in operating the Dojo so that Dojo coaches can put their energy where it matters most: developing the team.

You will see the Dojo Roadmap mentioned many times throughout this book.

This chapter will walk through the Dojo Roadmap through the eyes of a Dojo coach. That means taking a deep dive into each phase of the roadmap and expanding on coaching scenarios, points of consideration, caveats, and best practices.

The Big Picture Is Important

The big-picture view of anything is compelling because it alleviates anxiety through its inherent transparency, which helps people connect the dots. So let's start with it!

The Dojo Roadmap (Figure 2.1) begins with intake. Intake is where Dojo coaches evaluate the compatibility of teams to determine how suited a given team is for the Dojo. This process tends to take anywhere from one to three weeks.

Second, the Dojo Roadmap takes us into the Pre-Dojo phase. During Pre-Dojo, the selected Dojo team and the Dojo coaches work to set the Dojo engagement up for success by participating in exercises like defining Dojo goals. This process tends to take a half or full day.

Once intake and Pre-Dojo have been completed, we begin the Dojo engagement itself. The Dojo usually lasts around six weeks. Throughout this book, I demonstrate why a minimum of six weeks is important.

Following the Dojo, we begin the Post-Dojo phase. In Post-Dojo, we measure the progress the team has made on their Dojo goals and prepare the team to self-sustain Dojo goals.

Finally, we have the Dojo Follow-Up. This phase occurs six to eight weeks after the Dojo with the purpose of checking in on the team to see if the progress made in the Dojo has been sustained.

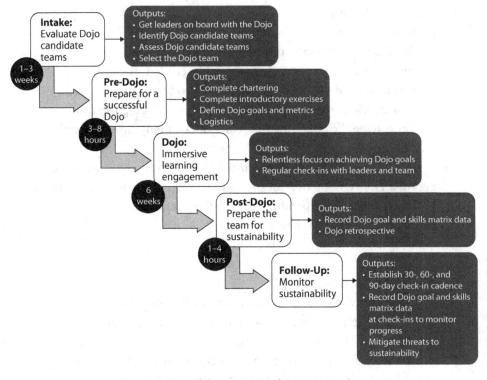

Figure 2.1: The Big-Picture View of the Dojo Roadmap

If the general flow of the Dojo does not seem familiar to you, you are encouraged to consult the introductory Dojo resources mentioned in the preface's "What to Expect from This Book" section before moving forward. You must have a base-level understanding of immersive learning Dojos in order to get the most out of this book.

Table 2.1 provides an example of the Dojo Roadmap in calendar form to give you a sense of scheduling.

Intake: Evaluating Teams for the Dojo

Key Outcomes of the Intake Phase

Not every team is Dojo compatible, so it is vital to determine a team's compatibility before starting a Dojo. The Dojo is new and shiny, and it is easy to jump into action without doing the proper assessment work (Figure 2.2).

Table 2.1. Dojo Roadmap Calendar

February	March	April	May	June	July
W1: Intake	W1: Dojo	W1: Dojo	30-day follow-up	60-day follow-up	90-day follow-up
W2: Intake	W2: Dojo	W2: Post-Dojo			
W3: Pre-Dojo	W3: Dojo				
W4: Dojo	W4: Dojo				

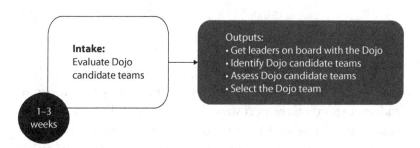

Figure 2.2: Key Outcomes of the Intake Phase

The last thing you want to do is place the wrong team in the Dojo. Doing that can burn out coaches, make the team resentful, and tarnish the reputation of the Dojo. As with most anything, it is quality over quantity. Trust me on this!

As a Dojo coach, you absolutely must make sure that both the teams and leaders you have introduced to the Dojo Roadmap understand that there is a chance they may not be selected for a Dojo. They should be made aware that the Dojo coaches select the most compatible team using methods that remove bias and support objectivity. Setting the expectation at the outset that they may not be selected will help avoid surprises and prevent hard feelings when delivering the news.

Because the news of rejection is a sensitive matter, I have provided a sample Dojo rejection email that has worked well for me. It offers a great starting point for delivering the news.

Dear team,

We are grateful that you let us into your team to explore how the Dojo may enable growth. More so, we admire your interest in improving as a team.

After a rigorous selection process, we're writing to inform you that we're going with another team for the next Dojo engagement.

Let's not leave it at that. During the Dojo intake process, we drew observations from your team, and we would like to set up some time with you to discuss them, with the hope that they may be deemed helpful in your pursuit of higher performance.

We look forward to hearing from you to continue the conversation.

Regards,

Jess

A Closer Look at Intake Operations

There may be some starting and stopping during the intake phase as you work to coordinate calendars and pause to hear back from leaders or teams on the next steps. But on average, Dojo intake consumes one to three weeks of a Dojo coach's total time per Dojo candidate team. In essence, the intake phase involves a couple of meetings (some with leaders and some with teams). However, the coach's team observations consume the most time during intake.

Getting Leaders on Board with the Dojo

Dojo intake starts with an introductory meeting with key leaders supporting the potential Dojo team or teams during their Dojo journey.

So what do I mean by "key leaders"? These generally include the team members' line managers, as they typically are responsible for helping their direct reports achieve professional development goals. For example, I have held introductory meetings with the technology line managers, who are over the team's developers, and product or business line managers, who are over the team's product owners or business analysts. Because the Dojo is a significant engagement, I have invited the senior leaders. There is no set formula for determining attendees because every organization has a different structure.

Table 2.2. Suggested Agenda for Dojo Intake Meeting with Leadership

Agenda item	Coach tip
What is a Dojo?	Leverage the "Dojo Introduction Slide Deck" (dojo pocketguide.com) to walk leaders through the core concepts of a Dojo. Following the core concepts, present the Big-Picture View of the Dojo Roadmap (Figure 2.1) to help bridge concepts to action. You'll want to check the attendees' understanding of the core concepts and roadmap before moving to the next objective. Book more meetings if needed. Do not rush this.
The value of Dojos	While the "Dojo Introduction Slide Deck" includes content on the value of Dojos, be sure to consult the chapter "Making the Case for the Dojo" for impossible-to-ignore value propositions.
The role of leaders in the Dojo	Leaders will not be active Dojo participants, but their role is vital. We'll learn why and how to deliver that message later in this chapter.
Next steps	It is important to provide transparency to leaders on what the next steps would be should they green-light the Dojo. Bring the Big-Picture View of the Dojo Roadmap (Figure 2.1) back up and show that the next steps will involve interacting with the candidate teams. The interaction will result in scoring each team to see how compatible they are with the Dojo. More on this later in the chapter.

However, do not be shy to invite high leaders or set up multiple introductory leadership meetings to ensure the right leaders are aligned on what a Dojo is and fully accept their role in the Dojo. This prework can define the success of a Dojo, so being methodical is a smart way forward. Table 2.2 provides a framework for conducting the intake meeting.

How to Approach the Introductory Meeting with Leaders This meeting is, first and foremost, a conversation. A real, honest, and, in some ways, tough-love-style conversation. That means you may call out unpleasant realities to support the urgency around developing people. That also means you will be actively listening about as much as you're talking, if not more.

Be mindful of lending empathy to the leaders as they process the Dojo for the first time. What you are presenting to them is a significant growth journey for their teams. It is appropriate for them to ask questions, hard questions. It can seem like they're poking holes in the Dojo. This is a good sign. If they're questioning the Dojo, that means they understand its significance and, most importantly, care about the organization, because they are not blindly stamping approval on it.

During my time as a Dojo coach, there have been a few Dojo leadership meetings where everyone in the room unanimously agreed to move forward with it. While that seems like the best day ever for a Dojo coach, it can mean that the group is susceptible to groupthink. Or they didn't really hear you.

Body language is a powerful indicator. We will often hold our palms out when we want to be open or honest. Check for that behavior. Also check to see if anyone's arms are crossed. If so, that almost always means they're defensive or skeptical and thus not sincerely sold on the Dojo. In remote meetings, do you see evidence of multitasking—that is, eyes drifting to other monitors? If so, that likely means the participant has lost interest.

Thinking back to recent introductory meetings I've held with leadership, most have been held remotely. Still, a coach can pick up on physical cues to determine sentiment. Midway through a remote meeting I was in, a leader placed both hands on his desk and pushed himself backward in his chair, increasing the gap between him and his camera. He then fell back in his chair and slouched. He seemed exasperated, yet he did not say anything even when I called on him for feedback.

I typically reach out to each leader individually for a quick check-in following the introductory meeting to explore their feelings toward the Dojo once they have had more time to mull it over. People often open up more in a one-on-one setting, especially if there isn't a big boss in the room creating a cloud of influence. In this instance, I am sure glad I checked in with the leader, because he happened to have strong feelings about the Dojo and needed time to organize his thoughts so we could have a meaningful discussion about it.

A good rule of thumb is that if something looks off, it probably is. Always trust your instincts.

If at first leadership reception is not strong, don't get discouraged. It may take more than one interaction to build their confidence in the Dojo. After all, it is a new concept that may be considered radical depending on the organization's existing culture.

Common Concern from Leaders about Dojos I think it is safe to say that the most widespread concern from leaders about Dojos is their team's availability during the Dojo. Often, when they hear "six weeks," they become anxious about their team being MIA for over a month. You can't blame leaders for this concern because as much as they want to grow their people, the truth is that if we take focus away from delivering value to the business, we're all in trouble.

With this in mind, you'll want to present the Impact of Dojo on Team Performance graph (Figure 2.3) to leadership so they can better understand what to expect in terms of the Dojo's impact on delivery.

In the next section, we'll talk about how the temporary dip in team performance turns out to be an investment that pays dividends in the long term.

Slow Down to Speed Up Sure, a main selling point of the Dojo is to learn by doing. However, let's not get fooled into naïveté: the Dojo engagement has been known to affect a team's delivery capabilities. In fact, referring back to the "Learning is greater than delivery" principle introduced in Chapter 1, we expect to see a dip in delivery during the first few weeks of the Dojo as the team acclimates to the high-touch coaching engagement.

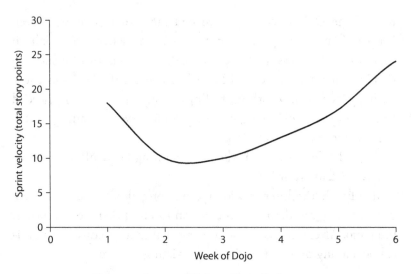

Figure 2.3: Impact of Dojo on Team Performance

In many cases, as the Dojo winds down, the coaching becomes lighter, and the team takes back the helm, they achieve a greater delivery capability than they had before the Dojo engagement.

A similar pattern can be observed in the work of Virginia Satir, a renowned psychotherapist specializing in family reconstruction. Specifically, her change model (Figure 2.4) is said to help guide people through the journey of significant change. Similarly, the Dojo brings significant change that disrupts a team's normal state. Satir's model appears to capture the impact of change within a Dojo engagement quite well.

- "Late status quo" is essentially the team's state before the Dojo begins. Weeks 0–1.
- "Resistance" resembles the trepidation many teams feel as the Dojo kicks off. It is like diving right into a pool versus dipping a toe. Weeks 1–2.
- "Chaos" is the part where performance slows down. This is when the team is finding its footing with new growth and acclimating to the new environment. Weeks 2–4.

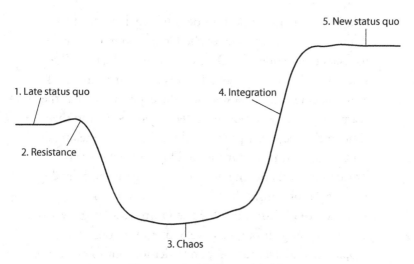

Figure 2.4: Satir's Change Model

- "Integration" is the milestone when the team starts seeing the new skills begin to stick within their context. Confidence starts to build as they are becoming increasingly independent. Weeks 4–5.
- "New status quo" is when the team has achieved growth, effectively improving their original status quo. Weeks 5–6.

The Satir change model portrays an improved status quo at the end of the change flow. This is important because the new status quo represents the return on investment from the Dojo. That is, the team has achieved sustained, long-standing growth.

The Role of Leaders in the Dojo Dojos need leadership's support. But not just any leadership and not just any support. The Dojo team's leadership must fully understand how to best support the Dojo experience.

Leaders should understand the three key commitments to enable the most valuable Dojo experience for their team:

1. **Commit to minimizing distractions for the Dojo team**—Leaders will be critical in shielding the Dojo team from unexpected work or distractions while the Dojo is in

progress, which is important because any break in focus dilutes the retentive value of the Dojo. Too many breaks in focus may render the Dojo completely valueless. The shielding can take whatever form is necessary. An email announcement to requesters sets the expectation that the team will only be responsive to emergencies during their time in the Dojo. Or perhaps all requests to the team get routed to the leaders during the Dojo. Whichever approach best suits the organization, erring on the side of more isolation rather than less isolation is the key.

2. **Commit to giving space for the Dojo team to grow**—If a team is going through a development program like a Dojo, it is understandable for a leader to want to be part of it. However, where there are leaders, pressure is usually placed on those who sit below them on the org chart. The pressure to appear smart and sharp consumes the vulnerability needed to learn something new, ask novice questions, or take risks. So to circumvent the risk of a constrained growth experience, it makes sense to remove leaders from the Dojo.

3. **Commit to actively participating in leadership check-in meetings**—Because leaders are not involved in the Dojo, we set up a cadence of check-ins throughout the Dojo (e.g., weekly or biweekly) so that leaders are still in the loop. The check-in with leaders is not exclusively for discussing the progress of the Dojo team; it is also an opportunity to ask leaders for assistance and to coach them on how to best support the team.

Getting acceptance from leaders on the three commitments is critical to the Dojo's success. It seems overkill, but even drafting a simple agreement for leaders to sign helps create accountability. There is no possible way to overstate the importance of leadership's role in the Dojo, so you, as the Dojo coach, must do what it takes to ensure the three commitments are well understood and accepted.

Identifying Dojo Candidate Teams

To manage the size of your Dojo candidate pool, it's helpful to define parameters. I like to call these knockout questions because they quickly filter out teams that do not meet the minimum requirements for a Dojo.

Table 2.3 lists a few knockout questions that I've seen used before. Disclaimer: These knockout questions are presented as examples only. Please use your discretion as to whether they apply to your Dojo. The intent behind sharing them is to inspire thought on how to identify compatible Dojo teams within your environment faster and more easily.

Assessing Dojo Candidate Teams

Once you've identified the Dojo candidate teams, the next step is to evaluate each of them to determine which one is the best fit for the Dojo.

The assessment phase begins with a meeting with the candidate team. The attendees of the introductory team meeting should be the knowledge workers, the product owner, and the Scrum master. Leaders are intentionally not invited to this meeting to avoid any influence or pressure that may come with their presence.

The first two objectives of the meeting are simple to address because they are no different from what you presented at the introductory meeting with leadership ("What is a Dojo?" and "The value of Dojos" in Table 2.2). However, the overall approach of the meeting with the team is different. Way different.

I've learned the hard way that you should request that leaders chat with the team about the Dojo first with the intent of getting their buy-in to learn more. This way, the team doesn't feel blindsided by the Dojo coach sending Dojo meeting invites to them. Only when the team agrees to learn more about the Dojo will they see the invite from the Dojo coach on their calendars. It is really hard to win people back, so take the time to do things right. Make sure transparency is at the forefront when interacting with new teams.

Table 2.3. Example Knockout Questions

"Yes" to any of these questions means Dojo disqualification.	
Question	Rationale
Is the team greater than 15 people?	According to the theory of Dunbar's number, the maximum number of close friendships humans can develop is 15.
Does the team consist of greater than 51 percent contractors?	The threshold is put into place because most organizations refrain from developing contractors—not out of spite but rather as a form of legal risk mitigation.
Is the team without a product owner?	The product owner is considered a team leader in product and Agile, so they must exist to help champion Dojo coaching.
Is the team without a Scrum master?	Who will get the baton once the Dojo coaches leave? The natural recipient is the team coach or team lead such as a Scrum master or manager. They are vital to keeping momentum on Dojo goals.
Is the team composed of individuals who have additional responsibilities outside the team?	For the Dojo to successfully build people, the people must be available and entirely focused.
Do any of the team members oppose the Dojo?	There must be 100 percent acceptance or nothing. Not having full approval from the team could dampen the Dojo experience, as bad attitudes tend to be contagious. Plus, it's just plain disrespectful to impose anything on anyone.

All of that said, let's pretend that we've made it to the team's calendars. You'll want to consider the initial meeting with the team an open conversation like that with leadership; however, psychological safety becomes significant. Assure them that "what happens here stays here."

I have seen various types of initial reactions to the Dojo. The majority of people seem warm to it and genuinely interested in learning how it may help them. However, I have seen a few other camps emerge, too. One seems to have anxious feelings such as, "What is wrong with this team that makes this person want to coach us?" or "I suppose the Dojo is a last-resort chance to get better so we can get out of hot water." Another camp is a bit more dismissive, showing feelings such as, "Why us? I don't see a reason to be coached." This reaction is usually rooted in the Dunning-Kruger effect, which means that an individual's inexperience renders them incapable of understanding their true abilities such that they do not know enough to distinguish between growth opportunities and ideal states, and therefore have a difficult time identifying the coaching needs they may have.

In any case, you must clearly articulate that the Dojo is not a form of rehabilitation. It is a catalyst for getting better in areas that are relevant to a specific team. It is where good teams become great. It's like my colleague says, "The Dojo is like Top Gun." Top Gun brings together the best pilots in the world to be coached so they can become better than ever. That couldn't be more true for the Dojo, as I've witnessed some of the strongest teams I've ever met in my career grow because of the Dojo. Every team has space to grow. Hell, if the greats like Simone Biles and Michael Jordan are not too good for coaching, no one is.

You'll want to be abundantly clear that the team ultimately controls their destiny; therefore, "no" to the Dojo is an entirely acceptable answer. The resistance is healthy and can signify a strong culture because the team feels empowered to think for themselves. If a team grows cold toward the Dojo, don't fret. Teams who initially resist tend to witness the success of other Dojo teams and become convinced by the evidence. And even if they don't, at least you can sleep at night knowing that there's a team out there owning it and doing things their way.

Ready, Willing, and Available I have found success in keeping the phrase "ready, willing, and available" top of mind as I assess Dojo candidate teams. What does it mean exactly? Well, it goes something like this: ready for learning, willing to grow and try new things, and available to participate—they've made mental space available to focus, and they're free from major deadlines or commitments that might disrupt the Dojo. Because the "ready, willing, and available" components are mostly subjective, you can't make it a knockout question. It is a gut feeling and an internal dialogue with yourself while engaging with the team. Dismissive body language such as slouching and signs of disengagement such as cameras being off or multitasking are surefire indicators that a team is not ready, willing, and available.

Why do we care about being ready, willing, and available? Well, a few reasons.

Bringing a team into the Dojo that is difficult to coach deprives a team that is better suited for the Dojo. Additionally, difficult coaching engagements, if not managed, can lead to burnout for coaches.

Signs of a Healthy Team Culture I strongly recommend reading *The Culture Code* by Daniel Coyle to gain a better understanding of what a healthy team culture looks like. Based on my experience in Dojo coaching, Coyle's content accurately reflects behaviors that I've seen in teams with strong culture. To give you a taste of what the behaviors are, Coyle says that "proximity, eye contact, energy, mimicry, turn-taking, attention, body language, vocal pitch, consistency of emphasis, and whether everyone talks to everyone else in the group" are surefire signs that the team has great chemistry.

Personally, I've found mimicry to be a strong signal. If I see team members match body language or use similar wording, it means they must choose to spend a lot of time around each other and their admiration is purposefully translated through behaviors.

If you are struggling with determining how to interpret a team's strong culture, consult Coyle's book for clear, tangible indicators that will make the decision easier for you.

What If Most Team Members Want a Dojo? You must gain the complete team's buy-in on the Dojo. "Complete" seems like a strong word choice, but it is appropriate. It is not good to pursue a Dojo if any team member disapproves of it. Yes, that means 100 percent acceptance. Not 98 percent or 99 percent. This is a must because the Dojo relies on *all team members* to achieve Dojo goals and sustainable growth. The Dojo is done as a whole team. The team gets uncomfortable together. The team unlearns together. The team makes breakthroughs together. It is all or nothing to keep the focus tight on the outcomes and free from the distractions introduced by internal conflict.

Anonymous polls tend to be a great tool for assessing the team's sentiments toward the Dojo. The poll does not need to be complicated; a single question such as, "Do you want to pursue a Dojo?" with the option for team members to select "yes" or "no" will do the trick. This is an easy way to encourage team members to respond honestly and get a true read of the team's sentiment.

Meet with the Scrum Master and Product Owner One-on-One As previously mentioned, meeting attendees can significantly influence the team's participation, conversation, and mood. It is essential to recognize that the Scrum masters and product owners generally want to appear as staunch allies of the team in front of the team, so they tend to be more reserved with their comments during Dojo intake. However, if you get them one-on-one, they tend to open up and tell you how things really are behind closed doors. What's more, because the Scrum master and product owner will champion the Dojo once it concludes, it makes good sense to begin developing those relationships early.

During the first meeting with the team, you should express the support from their leadership to engage in a Dojo. Team leaders should reach out to the team once they've initially met with the Dojo coaches. This provides the chance to open up if they were being too nice to the coaches, allowing leadership to reinforce their support with the team, particularly emphasizing the three leadership commitments that they've made:

1. Commit to minimizing distractions for the Dojo team.
2. Commit to giving space for the Dojo team to grow.
3. Commit to actively attending leadership check-in meetings.

Candidate Team Observations Assuming the candidate team is excited about the Dojo, the next step of the roadmap is to observe the team to get a first-hand understanding of its state and to validate any parameters you may have set for Dojo candidates.

The first thing you want to do is set the expectation of the observation with the team. The team should understand that the Dojo coaches are there to observe passively. They will not intervene to coach even if asked. The team is expected to operate as they usually would and ignore the Dojo coaches during the observation.

Next, an observation period should be defined. The recommended maximum observation period is two weeks or the length of a usual sprint. That should be plenty of time for the Dojo coach to glean insights from a team. In fact, sometimes a week's worth of observations is sufficient. At any rate, I recommend observing a team during an event-heavy week (e.g., a week that contains sprint refinement, sprint planning, a retrospective, or a demo).

An elephant in the room as it relates to team observations is that most teams are remote these days. Observing a team remotely comes with challenges, and we will cover how to navigate these challenges in the "WFH = Virtual and Hybrid Dojos" chapter.

What to Look for during Observations Your T-shaped skills as a Dojo coach, as described by Dion Stewart and Joel Tosi in *Creating Your Dojo*, shine as you look for antipatterns, powerful opportunities for improvement, and strengths to leverage within each Dojo candidate team.

From an Agile coaching perspective, you'll want to examine factors like the effectiveness of Agile events. If you are more of a technical coach, you'll want to check the team's Extreme Programming maturity and take a gander at their codebase.

Broaden your observations beyond practitioner perceptions. Take note of internal and external dependencies or hindrances and consider their impact on the team. For example, do you pick up on a pattern where a dependent team consistently pushes back user stories that affect the team?

Watch for team relationship dynamics as well. Do you notice any tension when a certain person joins a meeting, or do some meetings seem to be more easygoing than others? Does the group consistently become disengaged at a particular event or when certain people are present? Who's quiet? Who hogs the mic? I go back to body language again. Do people's words match their actions? In other words, when the team agrees on a story point estimate, are they *showing* that they agree? In *Like Switch*, psychologist and former FBI agent Jack Schafer claims that if you observe someone agreeing but pursing their lips, it likely means that they disagree. Subtle details can be big signs.

Observation Mindset Out in the field, I've witnessed checklists used for many things. Many, many things. They can be useful, game-changing tools, but I do not use them for observations. Why? Because key details are at risk of being missed due to mental energy being spent on checking the list.

Lyssa Adkins's iconic book *Coaching Agile Teams* is a must-read for any agilist. One of the valuable aspects is that it offers powerful team observation techniques. The book covers subjects like observation types and how to observe team conversations effectively.

Adkins suggests that our minds get "noisy"—the checklists are noise, in my opinion. Other noises could be anxiety about what the team will do next, a certain judgment about a team member, and many other thoughts. The noise distorts what's going on with the team at the moment. When the observer is present, a clear picture of what happened is obtained, which leads to advice and feedback for the team that has a more positive effect. To quote Adkins, "With presence, . . . you coach people from a place of certainty, you speak with clarity, and your words impact the team."

Another important component for strong observation comes from Laura Whitworth's book on co-active coaching, which covers thoughts on active listening. The book suggests that there are three levels of listening: internal listening (level I), focused listening (level II), and global listening (level III). Level I means that the words get interpreted through the listener's lens, where they are met with some version of themselves in the listener's head. In level II, the listener is freed from this personal lens, and the listener listens and responds at the moment, which helps the speaker move through what they are expressing. In level III, the listener uses everything in the environment, such as the speaker's voice and posture.

As a Dojo coach, it's imperative to stay at level III listening. It could make the difference between your observation notes reading, "Retrospectives have been lackluster and boring," and them reading, "It is a new team, so shyness is expected."

You may be an experienced coach who possesses vast empirical knowledge of team patterns. While that is a significant strength, it doesn't mean you can quickly jump to conclusions or make rash assumptions. You haven't coached this specific team within this particular environment and under these particular terms. As Adkins says, "Turn down your judgment and turn up your curiosity!"

An Ongoing Conversation The intake process is meant to identify teams that are the best fit for the Dojo, so it also identifies teams that are *not* the best fit for the Dojo.

It's easy to run off with the teams that fit the criteria for the Dojo and ghost the other teams that you have taken through the intake process.

Don't do that. Keep relationships warm with every team you've taken through the intake process.

- Every team that has gone through intake has opened up to you as the Dojo coach. They've laid everything out on the table, intending to get help. They were vulnerable with you, so to leave them coldly is insensitive.
- The intake process has served as an eye-opener. I have seen teams put in active effort to improve and become Dojo compatible. But you wouldn't know that if you weren't engaging with them.

- For the sake of good networking, you never know if an incompatible team may connect you to the next rock-star Dojo team.

All it takes is a 30-minute check-in quarterly or biannually (calendar reminders go a long way!). This is a low-effort way to create a big impact for your Dojo and to ensure you are valuing people first.

Selecting the Dojo Candidate Team

"All of our teams are Dojo compatible. How do we prioritize them?"

First of all, congratulations on having a great problem in your organization! Having a healthy backlog of teams fit for the Dojo is a spectacular place to be and a sign of broader strengths across the organization.

The best way to approach this problem is to create a fair and un-biased way to rank the teams. You wouldn't want to develop a per-ception of favoritism, which will ruin the Dojo's reputation. Plus, it's garbage ethics.

A straightforward way to rank Dojo candidate teams is by creat-ing a set of criteria that align with your organization's vision and picture of success. When all criteria are evaluated, each team will come away with a total number of points. Essentially, the team with the most points is at the top of the Dojo backlog, the team with the second-most points is in the second spot of the Dojo backlog, and so on, resulting in a natural prioritization as depicted in Table 2.4.

Table 2.4. Dojo Backlog

Team name	Total points
ACE Team	56
Orange Iguanas	53
Scrum & Coke	50

Table 2.5. Example Dojo Team Ranking Criteria

Criteria	Points if "yes"	Rationale
Is your Scrum master 100 percent dedicated to your team?	+5	Having a 100 percent dedicated Scrum master helps provide continuity to the Dojo.
Is your product owner 100 percent dedicated to your team?	+5	Having a 100 percent dedicated product owner helps provide continuity to the Dojo.
Is the team at risk of reorganization?	−10	Because Dojo teachings are centered on a team in their environment, if that changes soon after the Dojo, it erodes effectiveness.
Does the team usually make space for innovation or trying new ideas?	+10	It is good to have culture criteria because they are harder to achieve and thus better for ranking.
Does everyone on the team have what they need to perform their work (e.g., sufficient account access, code repositories, messaging apps, work tracking apps)?	−10	If team members do not have access to the proper tools, then the effectiveness of the Dojo would be diminished, unless we can determine a Dojo goal around adopting a new tool.

I have provided a "Dojo Team Scoring Guide" at dojopocket guide.com. It's meant to get you started in the Dojo team ranking process and is intended to be adapted to your needs. However, to get an idea of what the ranking criteria might look like now, Table 2.5 provides some examples.

Note: Please interpret these Dojo team ranking criteria as examples, not prescriptions. You will need to adapt the criteria to best suit your organization.

I have had success with using objective ranking to support Dojo team selection. Coupled with the knockout questions previously mentioned, it gives me some peace of mind knowing that I've been methodical in determining if a team is a fit.

Furthermore, for the teams that are not a good fit, the insights we gain from the Dojo candidate assessment provide them with factual findings to leverage in their pursuit of becoming a higher-performing team.

Pre-Dojo: Setting Up for Success

Key Outcomes of the Pre-Dojo Phase

At this point, you've selected a Dojo-compatible team by completing the intake phase of the Dojo Roadmap. A huge milestone, so great work, Dojo coach!

Next, you'll want to get right into preparing the Dojo for success by initiating the Pre-Dojo phase.

The essence of the Pre-Dojo phase is to align the team, the team's leadership, and Dojo coaches on what a successful Dojo experience resembles. Sounds clever, but what does that mean exactly?

The Pre-Dojo phase involves some work. But it is a worthwhile effort that ends up being an investment that supports the quality of the Dojo experience. The key outcomes of the Pre-Dojo phase are (1) agreeing on how everyone—the team, Dojo coaches, and leadership—will best work together during the Dojo; (2) taking an inventory of the technology stack to help identify opportunity areas; (3) creating the skills matrix; (4) defining what goals the team will work on during the Dojo; (5) defining how we will measure progress toward said goals; (6) baselining metrics so we can track progress; and, of course, (7) general logistics (Figure 2.5).

Typical Duration of the Pre-Dojo Phase

I've witnessed Pre-Dojo work consume a few hours or be broken up over a couple of days. Given the key outcomes of Pre-Dojo, I feel that a range of three to eight hours is a fair estimate.

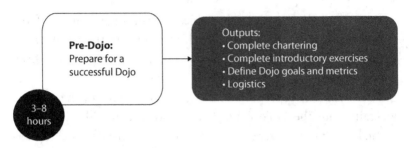

Figure 2.5: Key Outcomes of the Pre-Dojo Phase

An important note: it's easy for time to fly by when you have so many activities packed into an agenda, so you'll want to be mindful of breaks. A good rule of thumb is to set up breaks at least every 60 minutes regardless of whether the Dojo is in-person or virtual. That way, participants can do a mental reset and reengage properly.

Table 2.6 provides a suggested agenda for Pre-Dojo activities. This section will follow it as a guide and advise how to best approach each activity.

Defining the Dojo Working Agreement

As coaches, we're familiar with working agreements. We've used them, facilitated their development, and preached their value.

There is no doubt that working agreements have become ubiquitous in Agile because when they're used correctly, they serve as an excellent alignment tool for team members to understand how they best work together.

When it comes down to it, a Dojo working agreement is fundamentally the same as a team working agreement; however, there are a few points of distinction—namely, the Dojo working agreement is confined to the Dojo engagement, and it involves input from Dojo coaches who are external to the team, not the team exclusively.

I recommend setting up the working agreement session as you normally would. If you use a specific working agreement exercise or duration, feel free to roll with that. Ultimately, the goal of the Dojo working agreement is to define what the team and Dojo coaches need to succeed with the Dojo engagement.

Table 2.6. Suggested Agenda for Pre-Dojo Activities

Agenda item	Rationale
Dojo Roadmap review	Chances are, a good amount of time has passed since the team's intake activities. So it's a good idea to review the Dojo Roadmap as a refresher. This is a great way to get everyone's head in the game.
Introductory icebreaker	You'll want to get people loose and comfortable and create an opportunity to start building a rapport with the Dojo coaches. Most icebreakers will work fine, but I've had a lot of success with "Two Truths and a Lie" because it usually generates fun and interesting conversation. Additionally, as Dojo coaches, it is important to meet one-on-one with each team member regularly to develop trust and rapport. More on that later.
Dojo working agreement	Similar to a team working agreement, the Dojo working agreement aligns with how we will best work together in the Dojo. This is important to establish early in Pre-Dojo. For example, what time of the week is off-limits for Dojo coaching? What is the preferred communication method during the Dojo?
Architecture and technology stack visualization	This serves as a great discovery tool to reveal interteam dependencies and opportunities for technical coaching in the Dojo. It also provides context to nontechies as to how they contribute to the organization's broader value stream.
Skills matrix creation	The skills matrix provides visibility into the team's skill strengths and gaps, as well as providing a great tool for measuring the effect the Dojo has had on the team's skills. The architecture and technology stack exercise helps populate the skills matrix.
Dojo goals definition	Dojo goals serve as the overall theme of the Dojo, which dictates what will occur in the Dojo and how it will align with the team's success. Therefore, the quality of the Dojo goals affects the value of the Dojo.

(continued)

Table 2.6. Suggested Agenda for Pre-Dojo Activities (continued)

Agenda item	Rationale
Dojo goals measurement definition	In order to determine if we are making progress toward Dojo goals, we must define how we will measure progress. This activity is important to show the value of the Dojo.
Baselining Dojo goals	Baselining is standard practice when measuring goals. We must take a snapshot of where we are now to see if we've moved forward in the future.
Logistics	This is where we establish the Dojo schedule, core hours, general availability, and so on.

The following are some good Dojo working agreement responses from teams:

- Let's keep Dojo time inside this window: 12:00 p.m.–4:00 p.m.
- Be honest about what is or isn't working.
- There is no such thing as a bad question.
- Remain mindful about value delivery back to the business.

The following are some good Dojo working agreement responses from Dojo coaches:

- Engagement is critical. Close laptops and phones. If remote, turn webcams on.
- To maximize our time together, please be open to trying new things (even if it seems strange).
- Prioritize Dojo sessions. If something overlaps on the calendar, please favor the Dojo.

Visualizing the Architecture and Technology Stack
Because we'll be working from the team's backlog in the Dojo, it is important to understand the architecture and technology that power their product.

Table 2.7. What Tech Skills and Expertise Do We Need?

What we support	Language	Database
Account Service	Golang	MongoDB
Inventory Service	Golang	MongoDB
Shipping Service	Golang	MongoDB

With the architecture and tech stack visualized, Dojo coaches can help guide the conversation toward areas of opportunity. For example, we may point out that the team's core application has opportunities for improvement in the monitoring and logging space. From that, we'll begin thinking about external dependencies, such as needing to go through a permission request process to get access to these tools. The exploratory conversation is a great way to discover caveats ahead of the Dojo to enable a better-quality Dojo experience.

It's easy to go down a rabbit hole in the architecture and tech stack session, so start a basic table that captures the tech stack at a high level to get the ball rolling (Table 2.7).

After the table is defined, it is useful to sketch out the architecture. Again, less is more. A core reason for visualizing this information is to drive the conversation. Here is a basic architecture diagram for a fictitious storefront application (Figure 2.6) so you can get an idea of the level of detail that generally works well for this type of context-building session.

You can take this visual a step further by overlaying the technologies that are used for each part of the architecture (e.g., add MongoDB over the database symbols).

I advise against using existing technical diagrams instead of conducting this session, no matter how good they seem. That is because the actions involved in visualizing the architecture and tech stack spawn valuable conversation, curiosity, and exploration that can provide breakthroughs for a better Dojo.

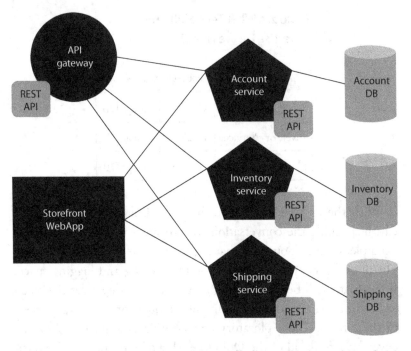

Figure 2.6: A Simple Architecture Diagram Is a Fast Way to Understand How a Team's Tech Works

Also, during the session, be sure you call on every technical person on the team to contribute (contractors, too). It is easy for a tech lead or senior engineer to hog the mic, and while that passion is incredible, it can stifle diversity of thought and stunt engagement from other team members.

Creating the Skills Matrix

If I had to say what I thought teams liked the most about the Pre-Dojo, it would only take three syllables: skills matrix.

The skills matrix provides unparalleled visibility into skill gaps and skill strengths on a team, which is extremely valuable for the team to know as they consider learning opportunities. The skills matrix has also helped motivate leadership to invest more in people development or create additional job requisitions to help better support teams.

Table 2.8. Example Skills Matrix

	Angular	MongoDB	Golang	Jenkins	Story writing
Stevie	3	2	1	1*	1*
Tracy	1*	3*	3*	3	1
Mick	0	0	0	0	3*
Janis	2*	2	1*	1*	3

Notes: 0 = not applicable; 1 = novice; 2 = intermediate; 3 = proficient. An asterisk indicates interest in the skill.

There is so much to gain from the skills matrix, yet they're easy to make! Especially because the preceding architecture and tech stack session provides a great base for identifying necessary skills to enable success for the team.

For a basic (yet powerful) skills matrix, all you need is the team members' names, any skills relevant to the team's success, and a rating system so individuals can self-rate their skills. As a bonus dimension, I also recommend including the ability for individuals to indicate skills that personally interest them. This encourages individuals to choose their own destinies and reiterates that they should be empowered to pursue their personal skill ambitions.

Table 2.8 provides an example of what a skills matrix looks like.

Most people's minds go straight to the rating scale for a variety of reasons. It makes total sense since you are telling your team how you perceive your abilities. "I don't want to seem arrogant, but I feel I'm proficient." "Wait—what do these ratings really mean?" As you can see, the skills matrix exercise can become overwhelming, so it is important that the Dojo coach defines parameters before conducting the exercise.

1. Honesty is everything; if we fail to rate honestly, then we compromise the outcome.
2. Assure the team that these ratings are not shared outside the team, as they are only relevant to the team.

3. Ensure the team is clear on what the ratings mean:
   a. "Not applicable" means it does not apply to you.
   b. "Novice" means you require guidance to perform it.
   c. "Intermediate" means you can perform it without guidance.
   d. "Proficient" means you are competent enough to teach it to others.
4. Last but certainly not least, when in doubt, ask the Dojo coach.

Another part you'll notice is that we went with specific skills over broader topics such as DevOps. That's because broader topics can lead to ambiguity, which may dilute the perceived value of the Dojo. In other words, what part of the DevOps spectrum did we upskill? There is a big difference between continuous integration and microservices, so don't leave people guessing.

Take note that I've included nontechnical skills. Hence, Mick, the Scrum master, has indicated "not applicable" for every skill except story writing. Any skills that enable success for the team are within scope. I've seen a column designated for internal communication before—whatever skills work for the team and context.

Additionally, I've found using numerical values for skills matrix ratings makes things more accessible while still keeping the intrinsic value of the exercise intact. You add or subtract or average fairly quickly with simple numbers to glean powerful insights about a team's skills.

The example skills matrix in Table 2.8 is basic and small. In real life, you could have a dozen or more skills listed. Nonetheless, the example demonstrates the powerful visibility that the matrix provides. Even in this basic example, the skills matrix lends insights, such as that Tracy is the only person on the team proficient with Jenkins, or that there appears to be a sizable chasm dividing the team's story writing competency. Insights such as these provide tremendous fodder for developing transformative Dojo goals.

Skills Matrix Cadence

Recording the team's skills matrix ratings during the Pre-Dojo phase, during the Post-Dojo phase, and during the Dojo Follow-Up session is important for demonstrating the growth that occurred in the Dojo.

Let's establish results expectations around the skills matrix and the Dojo. Radical transformations don't happen in a matter of weeks. For instance, junior developers do not metamorphose into senior developers; however, they could start contributing more confidently. They could develop a foundational understanding of a concept that leads them to skill breakthroughs beyond the Dojo.

Lastly, on the topic of cadence: the skills matrix is not just for Dojos. I'll repeat for those in the back: the skills matrix is not just for Dojos. So encourage Dojo teams to carry it on and revisit it using a regular cadence (quarterly or biannually), to keep skill development relevant in the team's conversations.

Defining the Dojo Goals

The Dojo goals are the heart of the Dojo. That's a big statement, but it's not hyperbolic. Everything we do in the Dojo is meant to drive progress toward the Dojo goals. What are Dojo goals, you ask? They are growth objectives (chosen by the team) that are reasonably achievable during the Dojo engagement. Following the "reasonably achievable" theme, I recommend not going further than three or four Dojo goals so the team's focus is not spread too thin.

The Dojo goals session itself is not difficult to facilitate. Essentially, you ask the team to collate possible areas of focus. You may break the team into groups or leverage facilitation techniques such as "1-2-4-All" from Keith McCandless and Henri Lipmanowicz's Liberating Structures. Once you have all the ideas generated, consolidate duplicate ideas and walk through each idea to ensure the group understands it. From there, a simple dot voting session does the trick for narrowing down the top three to four Dojo goals.

Sourcing Dojo Goals At this point on the Dojo Roadmap, there have been multiple opportunities to identify growth opportunities for the team. For instance, as the Dojo coach, you observed the team during the intake phase, which may be valuable to this conversation. Of course, you wouldn't want to impose Dojo goals, but it is good to share them with the team, given your expertise and unique vantage point. Opportunities appeared during the architecture and tech stack session and the skills matrix session. These findings are valuable to the Dojo goal definition, so it is crucial to have them visible while the team works through the Dojo goal exercise.

One more important factor to consider is the broader goal of the organization. Say the organization is looking to modernize legacy software. We'll want to consider skills that align with that outcome. Perhaps it's mapping out the move to microservices or upskilling engineers in Docker.

Recipe for Good Dojo Goals There are many books out in the world that talk about goal setting and goal measuring. If you search for "books about SMART goals" on Google right now, millions of results will appear. Within the millions of results, you are sure to find value; however, there is a straightforward recipe for Dojo goals that works well on its own.

Recipe for Dojo goals: one part clarity and one part balance. That's all there is. I'll explain.

Dojo goals need to be clearly understood by every member of the team. It's an obvious point, but an important one. Even after they are set, walk through the goals regularly (daily, if you can) to ensure that everyone is focused and unified in their interpretations of the Dojo goals.

The specific balance I am speaking about is attainable and ambitious. You don't want the team to give up hope on the Dojo goals, yet you don't want the goals to be too easy, because where's the growth in that? The following are some examples of good Dojo goals:

- Reduce the time of the production release cycle.
- Define a rhythm to consistently complete all stories in our sprints.

- As a team, become independent in Docker to reduce external dependency.
- Reduce the length of code reviews to decrease cycle time.

You may notice that none of these goals are timebound or measurable, which is a standard set by the ever-popular SMART goal convention. For example, a measurable and timebound version of the production release Dojo goal would be, "Reduce the time of the production release cycle by at least 10 percent before the Dojo concludes." From my personal experience, as soon as you associate a specific target with team goals, it invites concessions and gaming to prove the target. Thus, the focus is diverted from the actual outcome and sustainable growth. It is easy to become fixated on a shiny near-term prize.

Keeping the production release goal untethered to a specific target makes individuals more likely to find sustainable paths to growth as they're focused on becoming better than yesterday and developing long-standing habits.

Measuring Dojo Goals

Great! You have defined solid Dojo goals. But how do we know if progress is being made toward achieving the Dojo goals? We must define a way to measure progress, of course.

Baselining is fundamental to measuring progress because we need to know where we started in order to appreciate how far we've come. As a group, you will define the metrics along with each Dojo goal (for an example, see Table 2.9). Then capture the baseline data during Pre-Dojo. Do not go into the Dojo without baselining metrics for value integrity purposes.

You will capture data two more times in addition to the Pre-Dojo capture.

The second capture is at Post-Dojo, when you are winding down the Dojo. I've found this exercise is a great way to close the Dojo journey because it is like graduation. We've worked hard to improve the baseline metrics, and this is the first time we get to see how we've

Table 2.9. Examples of Dojo Goals with Measurements

Dojo goals	Metric	Pre-Dojo (baseline)	Post-Dojo	Follow-Up
Reduce the time of the production release cycle	Average time between code commit and production release	10 days	5 days	5 days
Define a rhythm to consistently complete all stories in our sprints	Sprint commitment versus completed	68%	88%	93%
As a team, become independent in Docker to reduce external dependency	Collective Docker rating on skills matrix	6	9	10
Reduce the length of code reviews to decrease cycle time	Average time a story remains in the code review column	6 days	2 days	2 days

progressed as a Dojo. It is a gratifying moment with camaraderie, indeed.

The last data capture is during the Follow-Up session and is the most critical measurement point. Why? Because the measurements at the Follow-Up session will show whether the team could sustain growth on its own without a Dojo coach's involvement.

One more thing about Dojo goals. Keep them visible. Keep them known. Refer to them as frequently as possible (standups are suitable for this)—hinge conversations, energy, focus, collaboration, memes, and *everything around the Dojo goals.*

Note: The Dojo Consortium (dojoconsortium.org) has excellent information about Dojo metrics.

Logistics

Ah, yes! Planning and coordinating calendars. Everyone's favorite activity! Okay, enough sarcasm. Logistics for the Dojo do not have to be hell on Earth for the Dojo.

1. Refer to any preferences defined in the Dojo working agreement (e.g., keep Dojo time between 12:00 p.m. and 4:00 p.m.).
2. Gather any out-of-office time for the team members (e.g., vacations, prescheduled events, public holidays).
3. As the Dojo coach, monitor Dojo logistics daily because the loss of a day can be significant.

Transitioning Pre-Dojo into Dojo

I tend to agree with Dion Stewart and Joel Tosi's suggestion in *Creating Your Dojo* to time Dojo prework no more than two weeks before the Dojo start date.

Simply put, the greater the window between Pre-Dojo and Dojo, the greater the risk of changes to the team's environment that could affect the prework. Factors like changing priorities or people changes have happened during this window, and if the changes are significant enough, they could render the Pre-Dojo efforts useless. And no one likes rework!

Further, by moving directly into the Dojo, you can seize the momentum generated from the Pre-Dojo activities. In other words, you've just amped up the team and made them hungry to achieve really cool and really tangible goals. Don't let that energy wane— keep them hungry for learning!

Dojo: Maximizing Effectiveness

Key Outcomes of the Dojo Phase

You've made it through all of the prework, and now you are ready to start the Dojo. This is where learning and growth will take place. This is what makes you a Dojo coach (Figure 2.7).

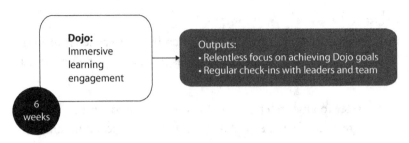

Figure 2.7: Key Outcomes of the Dojo Phase

Before we dive in, I cannot stress enough that the Dojo engagement is incredibly dynamic, so there is no bulletproof way to provide recommended agendas, templates, or processes as I've done in other sections of this book. Instead, I aim to provide empirical insights that focus on approaches and outcomes that will inspire you to maximize your unique Dojo engagements.

How Long Should Dojos Last?

Short answer: six weeks.

The six-week standard came from *Creating Your Dojo*, by Stewart and Tosi. The original Dojo practice that I was a part of did not challenge the standard of six weeks and instituted it right away.

Despite the blind faith, I must say I have not been displeased with the duration. It has proved to provide enough time to develop trust with the Dojo team and put them on a path of real change while not burning out the team or the coaches.

As much as my analytical mind hates to say this, I cannot find any scientific evidence supporting the six-week Dojo standard, even after reaching out to the authors of *Creating Your Dojo*. The success of the six-week standard seems to be a lucky coincidence, and, hey, there's no shame in accepting that.

Sure, I've adjusted Dojos to add on a week or two in a few cases where it made sense due to scheduling constraints or to avoid disrupting the team if they're rounding a corner on a breakthrough.

Can a Dojo engagement be shorter than six weeks? No. I've made "six-week minimum" a Dojo coaching principle for very good reasons.

Consult Chapter 1 or the FAQs section for a detailed rationale. However, if you don't feel like flipping pages, the TL;DR version is that it significantly impairs the value of the Dojo.

How to Approach Dojo Coaching

Every Dojo has different goals and dynamics, so, as I stated before, there is no way to develop a good template for what to coach. However, how to approach coaching in the Dojo is something we can explore further.

The Dojo is designed to generate rapid evolution. This means as a Dojo coach, you have to be scrappy and light on your feet to achieve a successful Dojo. What you planned yesterday may no longer make sense today. For example, let's say that a couple of days before, you planned a mobbing session to pull in a new set of API data. You see that access to the API has not been granted yet. You must now think quickly of a suitable pivot so that the time with the team is meaningful to the team's Dojo goals. Canceling or rescheduling is not an option because the Dojo is time-limited, and you need all the time you can get with the team. You must maximize every interaction with the team.

I use "rapid evolution" as a criterion for recruiting new Dojo coaches. Rapid evolution commands deep experience, grit, risk taking, and confidence. It is a tall order, and therefore it is not for everyone.

Many Dojo coaches (including myself) have served as some version of an Agile coach. That can make it difficult for us to fight old habits in our Agile coaching behaviors like delivery enablement. For instance, it can be hard to keep the focus on coaching toward Dojo goals when you see deficiencies in the value stream. But as Dojo coaches, we must remain disciplined about prioritizing learning. Everything else comes behind learning, including delivery.

That brings us to the concept of coaching for learning. Coaching for learning means that the intent of the coaching is keenly focused on growing an individual's knowledge or skillset.

Here is a fictional scenario that exemplifies coaching for learning:

DOJO COACH: *Hi, Jane. How's it coming along with your local instance of Docker?*

JANE: *Slow, but I think I finally got connected to Docker.*

DOJO COACH: *It sounds like you are progressing, which is great. How would you feel if I stepped in to help speed things up?*

JANE: *Yes, please! I can't wait to have the containers set up to have a fully functioning local development environment.*

DOJO COACH: *I'd be glad to, but I will simply be there to guide, as you know. You will be doing the doing. I propose that I help navigate as you drive, and I will stop at key points for us to discuss and document. Sound good?*

JANE: *That sounds perfect. I am excited about becoming self-sufficient. Who knows? I may help others with Docker in the future.*

The Dojo coach didn't provide an answer or do the work but rather asked questions to enable Jane to learn through hands-on practice. The tie back to coaching for learning is that though having Docker installed locally supports delivery efforts, delivery was not the focus. Learning was.

Later in this book, the chapter titled "Don't Be That Dojo Coach" will get into how to avoid specific Dojo coach antipatterns in order to further support coaching for learning.

In *Creating Your Dojo*, Stewart and Tosi mention Ebbinghaus's forgetting curve theory as it supports the key components of learning retention: spaced repetition and the meaningful presentation of the information intended to be retained. The Dojo model addresses both of these components nicely.

In the Dojo, exercises are repeated frequently. I cannot think of a Dojo where I coached a practice only once. At the minimum, two practices (spaced far enough apart to demonstrate retention) are needed to confirm that the team's initial success was not a fluke.

I've found that the best way to create solid associations for the team, and their learning, is by assimilating myself as the Dojo coach into their environment. This means a Dojo coach should attend all meetings—standup, retrospectives, story planning, story refinements, and demos. If there is a show-stopping production defect, show up to support in the best way possible. Hold one-on-ones with each team member and get to know them early on in the Dojo as you would if you were joining the team as a full-timer. The Dojo coach should do everything possible to position themselves as a team member. By being ever present, you are loading your coaching arsenal with insights to make Dojo coaching more meaningful to the team. Perhaps more powerful than that is the trust you are building with the individuals on the team. They will quickly respect you as someone who has a history in their environment (even if the history isn't long). After all, it's the mileage, not the years, that matters.

Coaching Intensity during the Dojo Engagement

Dojos wouldn't be effective in creating long-standing learning if they involved high-touch coaching from start to finish. Coaches must step back to see if the learning is sticking, and that is why we adjust coaching intensity (Table 2.10).

In the first three weeks of the Dojo, coaches need to be assertive, hog the mic a bit, demonstrate expertise, and provide hands-on

Table 2.10. Coaching Intensity during the Dojo Engagement

High touch: Coaches frequently intervene Medium touch: Coaches sometimes intervene Low touch: Coaches rarely intervene	
Week	Intensity
1	High touch
2	High touch
3	High touch
4	Medium touch
5	Low touch
6	Low touch

coaching. They are at the helm of setting a strong foundation for learning, so a high-touch approach is needed to get the dominoes moving.

However, by week 4, the Dojo coach should start stepping back a bit and only intervene to make corrections. This is called medium touch.

By weeks 5 and 6, the Dojo coach should not feel a need to intervene. The learnings should be part of normal practice—thus the low-touch designation.

Should You Adjust the Length of Sprints during the Dojo?

In *Creating Your Dojo*, Stewart and Tosi recommend 2.5-day sprints to foster retention through repetition. In theory, I adore this approach! In reality, 2.5-day sprints are too audacious for most organizations and have caused organizations to focus more on the sprint length than on learning. To counter the effects of the shock, I have led Dojos that tried one-week sprints. The shock wasn't as bad, but it still disrupted learning, and the team ultimately went back to two-week sprints after the Dojo.

So what do we do? I return to my earlier sentiment on assimilation: the Dojo coach should do everything possible to position themselves as a member of the team. That includes assimilating to the team's original sprint length. Or not enforcing sprints if the team doesn't already use sprints. The point is, I have not witnessed learning falter due to the length of the sprints in the Dojo. But I have seen sprint length mandates disrupt the Dojo.

Recommended Activities for Every Dojo

Table 2.11 provides a quick list of activities that I recommend as a standard for every Dojo.

The Samman Method: A Facilitation Pattern for Learning

Here is my shout-out to Emily Bache! She has created fantastic content related to technical coaching, and I have successfully incorporated her teachings from *Technical Agile Coaching with the Samman Method* into the Dojo.

Table 2.11. Standard Dojo Activities

Activity	Rationale
Psychological safety assessment	Vulnerability is needed to accept learning. Therefore, it is important to assess the team's overall psychological safety at the start of the Dojo engagement.
Working agreement creation or revisit Definition of ready creation or revisit Definition of done creation or revisit	Dojo coaches should be familiar with these documents so they have better context, but most of the time these documents are outdated or ill-formed, so a revisit serves as an opportunity to get them right. Furthermore, I've found revisits help teams get into the habit of regularly leveraging these documents, because they're often developed and then forgotten about.

Table 2.12. Samman Agenda

Objective	Duration
Learning hour: Overview of story splitting best practices	30 minutes
Ensemble working: Apply story splitting practices to stories in the team's backlog	60 minutes

The Samman method comprises two parts: learning hour and ensemble working. In the learning hour, the coach uses exercises and active learning techniques to teach the theory and practice of skills. In the ensemble sessions, the whole team collaborates with the coach to apply techniques in their environment.

The Samman method works well because shortening the distance between learning and application develops strong learning retention. Also, following a two-pronged approach to teaching creates variety. Too much lecture can be disengaging, and too much hands-on practice can be intimidating.

Table 2.12 presents the Samman method as an agenda.

I am not advocating using the Samman method for every Dojo activity; however, it is certainly worth keeping in your tool belt.

Weekly Experiments

A fellow Dojo coach inspired me to institute a weekly experiment on my Dojo engagements. These experiments are not time consuming and are meant to seamlessly plug into the team's workflow, and they are innocuous to Dojo goals.

Good weekly experiments would be walking the board from right to left in standup or timeboxing story refinements to 10 minutes per story.

Weekly (or regular) experiments bring additional value to the Dojo. They get the team practicing experiential learning and flexing their empowerment muscles, which greatly increases the odds of those behaviors becoming long-term habits.

Promoting Transparency

Kirsten Gillibrand stated, "I find that when you open the door toward openness and transparency, a lot of people will follow you through." That sentiment couldn't be more accurate in the Dojo.

The Dojo is new to most people who participate in it. The newness brings about natural trepidation, and that trepidation is prone to adversely affect the success of the Dojo.

Transparency is the surefire way to reduce trepidation and build trust and confidence, thus maximizing the effectiveness of the Dojo.

I've found that getting into a cadence of sharing a daily bite-size status of the Dojo with the team is a great way to promote focus and alignment. If team members can speak to what's going on in the Dojo daily, chances are they're building confidence in it. I've found that the easiest way to deliver the daily Dojo status is after the standup. I've even played it off as a news anchor for added amusement.

What's more, I've found that teams like to be informed of what's coming in the Dojo. You don't want to plan too far into the future because there are too many unknowns, so keeping planning to a maximum of one week is a good idea (Table 2.13). I've found that

Navigating the Dojo Roadmap ■ 51

Table 2.13. Dojo Schedule

	Monday	Tuesday	Wednesday	Thursday	Friday
	Analyze recent sprint performance	Regular sprint refinement	Set up local instances of Docker	Deep-dive production release process	Deep-dive production release process
Notes	*Dojo begins*				*Dojo continues*

the end of the week works well for revealing next week's proposed schedule. This allows Dojo coaches to capture last-minute updates from the current week and allows the team time to react to the scheduling proposal ahead of time. (Think: time maximization principle from Chapter 1.)

I learned about the weekly wrap-up in Stewart and Tosi's *Creating Your Dojo*. Essentially, it is a Dojo's version of a status update that goes out at the end of every week. It contains team wins, team impediments, progress toward Dojo goals, and next week's plan for the Dojo. The recipients include leadership and the Dojo team.

I am a fan of the weekly wrap-up, if it isn't obvious. It supports transparency and alignment for the team, the leaders, and the coaches. Moreover, as a Dojo coach, it creates time for reflection and helps keep the broader picture in mind as we round out another week in the Dojo. Here's an example of a weekly wrap-up email:

Subject: Dojo Week #3 Wrap-Up
Hello everyone,
We are rounding out another productive week in the Dojo! Here are the wrap-up details:

Wins:
- *All developers have participated in common types of paired programming. The stories that have been completed using pairing show an improved cycle time. This is a great early sign!*

- *The Scrum master applied advice from the Dojo coaches to adhere to the definition of ready in order to improve the effectiveness of the sprint planning session. The session ended on time for the first time in a long time, and the confidence around the sprint commitment was strong across the team.*

Impediments:
- *We are waiting to hear back about Docker access. If there is any way the leadership on this email could influence a quick response to our request, that would be great.*

Dojo goals progress:
- *Reduce the time of the production release cycle—On track*
- *Define a rhythm to consistently complete all stories in our sprints—On track*
- *As a team, become independent in Docker to reduce external dependency—At risk due to Docker impediments*
- *Reduce the length of code reviews to increase cycle time—On track*

Next week:
- *Set up and configure Docker on developers' local environments.*
- *Decide on ideas raised for reducing production release cycle.*
- *Continue pairing practice.*
- *Stretch: Begin practicing with Docker deployments.*

Establish a Feedback Mechanism for the Dojo Team

The Dojo engagement belongs to the team, and as Dojo coaches we should ensure that the team feels empowered to shape the Dojo engagement to best suit them. An excellent way to ensure the team is being heard during the Dojo is to establish a mechanism to share feedback with the Dojo coaches.

Adding a cadence to the team's Dojo feedback makes sure it is a prioritized activity in the Dojo. I have had success with requesting team feedback at the end of every week because it is not too frequent that it's burdensome and it is not too infrequent that improvements cannot be enjoyed. It also helps to see how the team's feedback week by week supports the team's overall Dojo story.

A simple web form with the capability of anonymity (e.g., Google Forms) is adequate for gathering feedback. At a previous Dojo organization, we took the value-rating approach. For example, on a scale from 0 to 5 (with 0 being the lowest rating and 5 being the highest rating), "How valuable is the Dojo for you?" You arrive at the value rating by averaging the team's responses. So if the ratings were 4, 4, 3, 5, 5, and 4, then the value rating would be 4.2.

Another field that is worth adding is an optional text area to capture any thoughts that the team is willing to share.

Let's say the team's feedback rating is a 5 for week 1, it stays at 5 for week 2, and then it plummets to 3.2 for week 3. This is not a far-fetched scenario because it has happened to me before.

The first step you should take as the Dojo coach is to identify why the Dojo is less valuable to the team. Have new factors been introduced? Is coaching not hitting the mark? In my case, it was the latter because the coaches overestimated the team's DevOps skillset. Luckily, our optional text area worked for us and we noticed a few comments that made it abundantly clear we were moving too fast. The team's feedback was completely valid as I reflected on the past couple of weeks. I recalled that we were getting right into designing the CI/CD pipeline and perhaps becoming too overzealous. I had a facepalm moment when I realized we had skipped rudimentary steps such as ensuring we had a shared understanding of what CI/CD meant and where to go for tooling access. Needless to say, we paused the Dojo immediately and worked as a group to determine the right balance of content and pace. One thing that came out of the collaboration was that the team found value in seeing what lesson was next so they could inform us ahead of time if it made sense or not.

Eventually, the rating returned to 5, and it stayed there for the remainder of the Dojo. While I love that part of the story, I must add that the learning that I gained from the experience was tremendous.

Where's Leadership during the Dojo?

Let's recall leadership's commitments to the Dojo earlier in this chapter. Leaders have committed to "actively participating in leadership check-in meetings." We intend to hold them to that. Leadership check-in meetings occur once a week during the Dojo. They are not a repeat of the weekly wrap-up, nor do they resemble a status update in any way. They are meant to ensure leaders are keeping true to their commitments to the Dojo, they are intended to ask for leadership's help if needed, and most importantly, they are intended to coach leaders on how to best support their team.

I would like to emphasize that last point. The leaders' receptiveness to coaching is a major contributing factor to the success of the Dojo.

During one of my first Dojo engagements, the team had warned me about the "neediness" of their leadership during the Pre-Dojo phase. From their description, the leaders did not consider the team's overall commitments and blindly threw things over the wall to them several times a week. The team wanted to please leadership, so they completed the ad hoc work alongside sprint work.

As you can imagine, this resulted in long nights, damaged morale, and quality issues. The Dojo began, and within days team members were receiving ad hoc requests. Worse, the requests bypassed the Scrum master and product owner and went straight to developers. Some leadership requests even contradicted one another. One leader would send a brief email asking for one thing, and another would submit a ticket asking for the exact opposite. It was abundantly clear that the leaders' antipatterns were harming this team, and a coaching intervention was necessary.

Fortunately, the leaders in this scenario were receptive to coaching and ultimately agreed to develop a leadership working agreement. The agreement included commitments such as, "Leaders will go through the product owner or Scrum master to request work," and "Leaders will not claim an emergency unless XYZ conditions are met." Thanks to the leaders' receptiveness, we were able to deliver a valuable Dojo experience.

Engage Anyone Who Can Influence or Be Influenced by the Team

A significant group of people that I have not touched on is the people who interact with the Dojo team and the Dojo team's leadership. Their feedback is often some of the most valuable during the Dojo because their position lacks bias and is usually outcome centered. They may not know what a Dojo is (which is entirely fine), but they'll know if something has caused an impact on the organization or a product offering.

Who are these people? Architects, user-experience specialists, embedded Agile coaches, dependent teams, and customers are excellent sources for external party feedback.

Apart from providing feedback, keeping these parties apprised of the team's Dojo journey helps create a supportive environment for the team so that the learning has a greater chance of sticking.

Post-Dojo: Supporting Self-Sustainability

Key Outcomes of the Post-Dojo Phase

As the Dojo coach, you've grown quite close to your team over time. Leaving them behind is tough, but you know that there's some preparation you can do for them to make them as successful without you there in person. This preparation is the essence of the Post-Dojo phase (Figure 2.8).

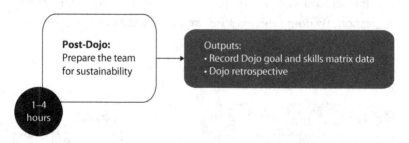

Figure 2.8: Key Outcomes of the Post-Dojo Phase

Capturing Dojo Goal Metrics

Back in Pre-Dojo, we defined metrics for each Dojo goal for base-lining purposes. It is now time to capture those same metrics again to determine progress (Table 2.14).

Bear in mind that since this is the first time you will be measuring the success of the Dojo, it is easy to get caught up in the numbers and fail to attend to the human aspect of the activity. Case in point, I've been a part of Dojos where the Post-Dojo goal measurements looked incredible, but in that same Dojo, if you were to ask team members about how they felt about the progress made on certain Dojo goals, they would not describe it as incredible. Take the time to have a conversation with the team about the results.

Another suggestion I have is capturing Post-Dojo metrics as the first step to the Post-Dojo phase, as it will help drive meaningful conversations about what self-sustainability measures could look like for the team.

Creating Momentum for Self-Sustainability

Now that we have captured our metrics, it's time to address any potential threats that may lead to regression. Before we address threats, we first need to define them.

I recommend TRIZ by Liberating Structures (the project of Keith McCandless and Henri Lipmanowicz) as an effective facilitation format for this exercise. TRIZ involves writing down all of the worst possible scenarios of something you're trying to avoid—in this case, regression. By doing this exercise, we gain clarity as a group on what to avoid and how to stay accountable.

Table 2.14. Dojo Goal Metrics

Dojo Goals	Metric	Pre-Dojo (baseline)	Post-Dojo	Follow-Up
Reduce the time of the production release cycle	Average time between code commit and production release	10 days	5 days	TBD

Also, it is not a bad idea to ask the team members to sign their names to the TRIZ activity as a gesture of commitment and accountability—to themselves and their team.

Lastly, keeping to good habits takes active discipline, so the team must keep monitoring threats relevant to their environment. Assigning the Scrum master to champion accountability works really well.

Dojo Retrospective

Feedback is welcome anytime during the Dojo; however, it is beneficial to reflect on the entirety of the Dojo engagement. The Dojo is not a typical work engagement. It can be very personal because we're addressing behaviors and habits, so it is nice to add proper closure.

During the retrospective, the Dojo coaches carry the team's feedback about the operations, facilitation, and coaching of the Dojo forward to improve the next Dojo. The team takes forward meaningful insights to continue refining their behaviors.

A fun way to memorialize the Dojo retrospective is to ask the team to advise the next team that goes through the Dojo. Or hold a Dojo graduation ceremony to kick off the retrospective to acknowledge each individual's Dojo journey properly.

Post-Dojo Logistics

Logistics vary for each Dojo but generally focus on transitional logistics. This could mean cleaning up any access that is no longer relevant to Dojo coaches, handing off access to team members who will be carrying something forward, or removing recurring events from calendars.

Also, this is an excellent time to book the Dojo Follow-Up meeting with the team. I recommend choosing a one-hour time slot about six to eight weeks out.

Follow-Up: Maintaining Long-Term Growth
Key Outcomes of the Follow-Up Phase

In my opinion, no matter how incredible a Dojo engagement may seem, we can only determine the success of the Dojo when we follow up with the team after the Dojo (Figure 2.9).

Figure 2.9: Key Outcomes of the Follow-Up Phase

Sure, there are breakthroughs and moments of progress during the Dojo. But if the team can exhibit sustained or improved growth after the Dojo on its own without the guidance of a Dojo coach, that means long-standing growth has been achieved; therefore, it is critical that the Dojo coach follow up with the team after the Dojo concludes.

Follow-Up Frequency (30, 60, and 90 Days)

A popular milestone scheme for employee onboarding is 30, 60, and 90 days, so it was one of the first ideas that came to mind when working with colleagues to form the Dojo Follow-Up frequency. Out of sheer coincidence, the frequency works well.

After 30 days, the Dojo is still somewhat fresh, and the team usually does a good job remembering the practices taught in the Dojo. There are usually comments like, "I've been doing X more, and actively try to stop myself from doing Y," or "I can hear the Dojo coach's voice in my head." Overall, the vibe of the session is light, and it feels good to see familiar faces again.

After 60 days, you start to see which practices are more likely to stick than others. Individuals fall back into their old habits, and the sheen of the Dojo could have faded for the leadership, too, so they may be reverting to bad behaviors. Common comments include, "I know better. What can I do to hold myself accountable?" or "I completely forgot about X that we worked on in the Dojo. I'll remember next time."

After 90 days it is easy to determine which success is long lasting and which is superficial. At this point, the team has been coached on their unique challenge areas for over four months, so if progress

Table 2.15. Dojo Goal Metrics (90 Days)

Dojo goals	Metric	Follow-Up 30 days	Follow-Up 60 days	Follow-Up 90 days
Reduce the time of the production release cycle	Average time between code commit and production release	5 days	5 days	4 days

is still not where it should be, there is no question that a course of action is needed to incite progress.

Capturing Dojo Goal Metrics throughout Follow-Ups

At each follow-up interval, we gather the same metrics we defined in Pre-Dojo so we can determine if the team is progressing—specifically, the metrics that were attached to each Dojo goal (Table 2.15).

As with the Post-Dojo phase, I recommend capturing data before discussing with the team because it serves as a conversation driver.

Pulling Insights from the Data

Let's say the team had strong growth between Pre-Dojo and Post-Dojo, but the growth declined from Post-Dojo to Follow-Up. Could this tell us that something in their environment is not working to support the Dojo's growth? Perhaps the decline was expected because people were out on leave. The only way to find out for sure is to engage the team to find the cause.

Success Is More Than Data

Yeah, sometimes data makes success seem obvious, but we need more than data to demonstrate the long-term success of the Dojo. Especially because data is notorious for being misinterpreted or manipulated (often unintentionally). There is a whole soapbox rant I could go on about misleading data insights, but I'll spare you.

The point is that higher team performance and improved individual behaviors cannot be supported by data alone.

Before my daughter was born in 2013, I was inspired to get in better shape. I invested in a personal trainer, a nutritionist, and a ton of coffee to get me through the 6:00 a.m. workouts. Very long story short, I ended up meeting my body fat and weight goals, but when my trainer followed up with me months after the program, he didn't ask for my weight and body fat percentage to determine if I had succeeded. He asked me more about the behaviors that supported my body fat and weight goals. For example, "How are you eating?" "How is the exercise regime now that you are on your own?"

The conversation is not so different in the Dojo. When you interact with the team at the Follow-Up, it is essential that you confirm signs of lasting change. Say a team has done a great job with keeping their Dojo metrics up. Have they found a way to make numbers, or are they applying what they learned and, as a result, the numbers look great? Get curious and keep *long-standing growth* as the underlying theme of the Follow-Up conversations. In all honesty, it should be the theme of every Dojo conversation.

If we do confirm that a team does not exhibit behaviors of long-standing growth, as Dojo coaches, we cannot sit idly by. The Dojo coach may be able to provide advice on the spot to get the team back on track. However, in other cases, it may take a few more sessions of meeting with the team and leadership to determine the root cause and strategy for overcoming it. In any case, speed is crucial in affirming or correcting behaviors because neural pathways are strengthened and become habits through repetition, feeling, and acting.

Follow-Ups for Different Audiences

I recommend hosting two separate Dojo Follow-Up sessions: one for leaders and one for the team. The reasons why are (1) continuity: the leaders have had a separate tangent going with the Dojo coaches, and (2) psychological safety: the team should continue to feel safe and not hold back feedback, and adding leadership may affect their ability to do so.

3 ■ Approaching the Dojo like a Product

The Dojo is a powerful skill-development model that has led to the rapid development of teams. While the buzz and success of Dojos are incredible, they also create blind spots and distractions that can hinder the progression of the Dojo itself.

Like products, Dojos must evolve to remain valuable in a digital-first world where technology, markets, society, and business continuously change. If we fail to grow the Dojo as we would a product, we risk diminishing its effectiveness. In a world where we need to work hard to keep learning programs funded, the Dojo must be vigilant about showing its value to remain a fixture in organizations.

Dojo Product Vision and Strategy

It all starts with defining the Dojo product vision and strategy. By doing so, alignment is achieved across the Dojo team and hypotheses emerge so the learning cycle can begin.

One of the simplest and most effective ways to define product vision and strategy is by running the Dojo through the Product Vision Board by none other than product expert Roman Pichler.

Figure 3.1 is a Product Vision Board inspired by Pichler with fictitious Dojo details.

- The vision is the ultimate reason for creating the Dojo. Why does the Dojo exist? Keep the vision memorable because it is meant to be shared beyond the Dojo team. The Dojo team will own this as their North Star.
- The target group for the Dojo is anyone who is likely to directly benefit from it.
- The needs part gets into the value proposition. What problems are being solved by the Dojo? What makes the Dojo valuable?
- The product section gets into the unique propositions offered by the Dojo that cannot be satisfied by other products.
- The business goals explain why it's worthwhile for the organization to invest in the Dojo. The goals address the organization's broader strategic objectives.

In addition to creating alignment within the Dojo team, the Product Vision Board is a powerful tool for communicating the intent and value of the Dojo externally.

It contains information that leadership finds valuable in a simple and clean fashion, which means it could serve as a springboard for conversations about business cases or defining the Dojo's place in the broader organization. In any case, it provides transparency to anyone external to the Dojo team, so they understand what the Dojo is striving for.

The Dojo Product Backlog

Now that we have alignment on the vision and strategy of the Dojo, we need to develop a product backlog for the Dojo product to identify and prioritize user stories that will develop the Dojo product.

VISION	What is your motivation for creating the product? Which positive change should it bring about?		Develop people in Agile, DevOps, and XP programming to enhance the capabilities of the broader organization.
TARGET GROUP	NEEDS	PRODUCT	BUSINESS GOALS
Which market or market segment does the product address?	What problem does the product solve?	What product is it?	How is the product going to benefit the company?
Who are the target customers and users?	Which benefit does it provide?	What makes it stand out?	What are the business goals?
		Is it feasible to develop the product?	
Developers and engineers looking to develop their technical skills	The Dojo aims to narrow the ever-widening skill gaps in technology and products that hinder the organization from meeting strategic objectives.	The Dojo is effective in addressing needs because it supports long-lasting skill development.	The Dojo responds to the organization's modernization goals by equipping people to effectively develop products in today's digital-first world.
Scrum masters looking to hone their coaching skills to enable higher-performing teams		A notable differentiator for Dojos is that they involve building skills while delivering on work.	
Product owners looking to hone their product-thinking skills to create powerful value for the organization	Additionally, professional development helps reduce turnover because people feel their learning journeys are valued.		

Figure 3.1: Example Product Vision Board

Naturally, you will begin adding user stories that support the Dojo vision and strategy. See Figure 3.2 to understand what I mean.

As a Dojo team, you'll want to determine a cadence for maintaining and delivering the backlog. This could be a traditional two-week sprint with refinement and planning. Or I have seen Dojo teams deliver backlog items in between Dojos so that they devote 100 percent of their attention to the active Dojo. The cadence is what's important, as it keeps the momentum going toward creating your most valuable Dojo.

In my experience, every Dojo engagement has resulted in opportunities for improvement. Of course, you'll take notes along the way when improvement areas crop up, but there are also weekly team check-ins, leadership check-ins, and the Dojo retrospective at the end of the engagement. They are all excellent sources for improvement ideas.

In fact, the Pre-Dojo team observations are an excellent example of a step that did not exist until we had a few Dojos under our belt. Initially, we would start Dojos cold with no prior history with the team. This meant that the first one to two weeks of the Dojo were consumed by the coaches' reconnaissance. Pre-Dojo team observations enabled us to develop a history with the team so that we were able to coach effectively from the very start of the Dojo engagement.

Additional Dojo Product Exercises

These exercises are not strictly required but have proved to help produce a valuable Dojo.

- Lean UX Canvas by Jeff Gothelf and Josh Seiden—The Dojo is not software that you can roll back if an idea falls flat, so the wrong idea can be difficult to correct. For that reason, be methodical about changes that have the propensity to be influential. Gothelf and Seiden's Lean UX Canvas is a great tool for crystallizing any hypotheses that may emerge as your Dojo evolves.

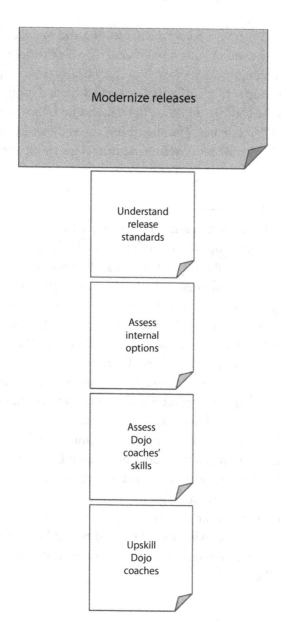

Figure 3.2: Dojo Product Feature with Associated User Stories

- Value Stream—I recommend creating and maintaining a Value Stream of your Dojo. There is so much goodness in visualizing the Dojo flow. Number one, it makes improvements easier to identify. It helps reveal them. Number two, the end-to-end flow can be useful for onboarding new Dojo coaches. Number three, the end-to-end flow may be valuable for external audiences for transparency.

Meaningful Dojo Offerings

The Dojo product vision and strategy exercise should provide a picture of what meaningful Dojo offerings look like in your environment. Meaningful offerings satisfy the skill development needs that enable strategically aligned objectives for the organization.

Let's say that the organization aims to increase innovation. The Dojo coaches assess their skills and experience to determine how they may teach skills that foster innovation, such as faster releases to enable speedier customer validation of ideas.

Building from the example scenario, meaningful Dojo offerings start to take shape in continuous delivery, automation, or alternative approaches to releases (e.g., canary releases).

But if Dojo coaches are unaware of organizational goals or technical standards, how can they form meaningful Dojo offerings? Well, they can't. That is why the Dojo practice should always be aligned with the organization's strategic objectives.

Table 3.1 provides meaningful offerings that I've seen in practice. Again, your offerings will most likely be different from what you see here, but I hope these give you an idea of what meaningful offerings look like.

Skills Matrix for Dojo Coaches

We discussed the skills matrix back in Pre-Dojo. It is a valuable tool for visualizing a team's competency in the skills needed to support their product. Why wouldn't we practice what we preach and apply the skills matrix to the Dojo coaches? It is an excellent way to drive

Table 3.1. Example Dojo Offerings

Offerings	Indicators
User story quality	• Team often does not have enough information to complete story • Rework is present • Prolonged UAT • Team is not clear on business value • Definition of ready is not present or not being met
Escalation management	• Leaders react to escalations, so groups are no longer working through product owner or Scrum master and there is confusion with the priority of work
Test-driven development	• Overly complicated codebase • Fear of making changes to some code • Fear of refactoring • Test cases are an afterthought • Instability brought on by connections between unrelated code
Application logging	• Widely distributed logs that make it difficult to stitch together a picture of what's happening • Too much noise in the logs compared with signals • Not enough detail in error logs to piece together the causes of errors • A lot of time is spent re-creating and debugging problems

Dojo coaches' development, so they are best able to deliver strategically aligned offerings and practices of the Dojo. Or it could prompt the team to hire additional Dojo coaches to fill skill gaps and strengthen Dojo coaching capabilities.

And again, revisit the Dojo coaches' skills matrix regularly (quarterly is usually a reasonable interval) and plan to address skill gaps to ensure quality is nurtured.

Table 3.2. Dojo Coach Skills Matrix

	Angular	MongoDB	Golang	Jenkins	Story writing	Leadership coaching
Aaron	2	3	3	2*	3*	3
Alex	1*	2*	1*	3	3	3*
Lisa	2	1	1	1	3*	2
Oren	3*	2	2*	1*	3	1

Notes: 0 = not applicable; 1 = novice; 2 = intermediate; 3 = proficient. An asterisk indicates interest in the skill.

The Dojo coach skills matrix (Table 3.2) should have similarities to the team's skills matrix because the Dojo coaches should be coaching skills that align to the organization's strategic objectives.

Types of Dojos

Today's Dojo landscape has grown and diversified into a myriad of different formats and styles. Each type promotes the "learn by doing" spirit, but their focus areas vary.

- Agile Dojos—Grow Agile mindsets and Agile practices to promote faster, iterative releases for better feedback loops with customers.
- Product Dojos—Address ways to optimize product value to customers.
- Innovation Dojo—Accelerate ideas to validate a minimum viable product.
- DevOps—Explore methods for shortening the release cycle to enable continuous delivery with high software quality.

There was a time not so long ago when these Dojo types did not exist. What Dojo type has yet to be discovered? With the booming interest in the decentralized web, might we see the concept of a Web3 Dojo come to life? Anyone's guess is fair—however, I am pulling for a Dojo for Dojo coaches.

4 ■ WFH = Virtual and Hybrid Dojos

Before COVID-19, a major contributing factor to the Dojo's success was collocation. Think hypercollocation—an open-space-concept room filled with whiteboard walls, oversize monitors, pairing stations, and busy collaboration.

But then the pandemic hit, and the worldwide lockdown suddenly became the Dojo's biggest roadblock. How could we maintain the effectiveness of Dojo engagements when we couldn't collaborate freely in person? How would we keep people engaged when they were simultaneously managing their home lives?

In early 2022, employers were slowly welcoming employees back into the office. This creates another challenge for Dojos: mixed-location or hybrid Dojos. How will we approach Dojos when part of the team is in-person and the other part is remote? Will it cause a divide in effectiveness?

As a Dojo coach who survived the switch to remote and the return to the office postpandemic, I am here to tell you I have successfully completed more virtual and hybrid Dojos than fully in-person Dojos. Let's face it: remote working is here to stay, which means the preference for Dojos will likely be hybrid or remote.

So throw on your headset, fire up your webcam, and unmute yourself for a chapter that divulges lessons learned from the trenches of virtual and hybrid Dojos, addressing the most common challenges and explaining how to overcome them.

Virtual Dojo Preparedness Checklist

First things first: Is the team capable of participating in a virtual Dojo? Take a look at the preliminary checklist I've compiled to help determine if a virtual Dojo is a viable option for a given team:

- **Does everyone on the team have a reliable and consistent, high-speed internet connection (i.e., no recurring connectivity drops)?** A straightforward requirement of remote collaboration, indeed. There are few things worse than suffering through a glitchy video call. Also, we don't have much time to spare in the Dojo, so rescheduling is a setback with a large impact.
- **Is the team made up of individuals who work within time zones that are greater than three hours apart?** Because Dojos are a full-team engagement, I've found that the Dojo experience becomes degraded if it means individuals work outside business hours to participate.
- **Does everyone on the team have access to video-conferencing and screen-sharing tools such as Zoom, Microsoft Teams, and so on?** Screen sharing and video conferencing are essential for effectiveness.
- **Does everyone on the team possess video-conferencing equipment—webcam, microphone, and speaker?** Participants will need to be able to hear, be heard, and see one another from their home office.
- **To access code, backlogs, or documentation, may the Dojo coaches have remote access to the organization's**

network using their own device or a device issued by the organization? The sky won't fall if a Dojo coach cannot get into the network, but making compromises like asking the team to screen-share to see the content within their network (if NDAs allow it) creates annoying overhead, and it does not allow the Dojo coach to perform reconnaissance, which yields significant insights for the team.

- **Does everyone on the team have privileges to access messaging tools such as Slack, Microsoft Teams, and Zoom?** Can a virtual Dojo exist without a messaging app? Yes. Will the Dojo be worse off as a result? Also yes. Messaging apps are good for focus and alignment because they keep the team plugged in on the Dojo happenings like a news ticker. Further, a messaging app does wonders for building camaraderie and morale in the Dojo. Some of my all-time favorite memes were discovered in a team's Dojo Slack channel.

- **Does everyone on the team have access to digital-first virtual collaboration boards such as Mural, Miro, and Microsoft Whiteboard?** Same as above. Virtual collaboration boards are not required to host a virtual Dojo, but they are game changers for creating interactive and effective learning sessions. I adamantly encourage them in the Dojos that I lead.

From my experience, I can confidently report that if a team satisfies the Virtual Dojo Preparedness Checklist, it will result in a successful virtual Dojo experience. But my experience may not reflect your context, so please use the checklist as a starting point for adaptation to suit your virtual Dojo practice.

Maximizing Virtual Engagement

In the in-person setting, maintaining participant engagement is the primary challenge for facilitators. Virtual Dojos (full or partial) are no exception to this challenge. In fact, it is my belief that virtual engagement challenges in the Dojo are exacerbated because the model was originally intended for full collocation. Let's explore ways to achieve high engagement levels for virtual and hybrid Dojos, equivalent to what we'd see in a collocated setting.

The first piece of advice that comes to mind for maximizing virtual engagement in the Dojo is to keep cameras on. I could argue that keeping cameras on for other sessions, such as large-format webinars or all-hands meetings, may not provide much value. But the Dojo is a world away from a traditional session—it's an intimate gathering with a timeboxed, value-driven purpose—and therefore the small act of turning on cameras goes a long way. For instance, Dojo coaches can read the room with the cameras on. They can pick up on real-time feedback such as facial expressions and body language that could indicate that the instruction is ineffective, enabling them to alter their teaching approach instantaneously.

In *The Remote Facilitator's Pocket Guide*, Kirsten Clacey and Jay-Allen Morris raise the issue of invisible group norms occurring in the virtual setting, meaning the instinctive norms that guide human behaviors are rendered invisible. For example, it is easier to sense if someone wants to speak if you see them breathe in, lean forward, or gesture. Many of our interactions are guided by intuition rather than overt rules as social beings. Keeping cameras on during the Dojo helps us preserve our natural social intuitions.

If you are hosting a hybrid Dojo, that strengthens the case for the camera because a first-class and second-class citizen divide is felt strongly when some team members are physically visible and some are not. That can manifest as deeper conflict and resentment. It is an easy problem to avoid and an even easier problem to let get out of control.

Another tip for virtual Dojo engagement is to set session expectations upfront. Shoot out a Slack message or email sharing the learning outcomes of the upcoming Dojo session. Also remind the team that they should plan to actively participate throughout the session and encourage them to turn off notifications and close other applications on their browser, so they are fully focused. This communication may take you five minutes to prepare and send out, but given that focus and engagement are critical ingredients for an effective Dojo, it is a worthwhile effort. Heck, this is a good practice for collocated Dojos, too.

Participation nurtures engagement. Setting the expectation that you will frequently call on the team to participate keeps them paying attention and focused during Dojo sessions since they know you could reach out to them anytime.

Encouraging participation can be as simple as using a prompt such as "Raise your hand if you've done this before," or "What is your biggest takeaway from this session?" Engaging in conversation with the group not only makes them personally invested, it has been known to blossom additional discoveries and questions. You don't know unless you ask!

Another form of participation is through breakout sessions. I enjoy breakouts because they give everyone the opportunity to participate.

The following are some tips for effective breakouts:

- Give clear and detailed instructions so the groups know exactly what to do in their breakout. Then call on one or two people from the team to repeat the instructions back in order to make sure they have been retained. Asking participants to parrot back the instructions is not meant to be condescending or embarrass them. Rather, it is meant to expose any misinterpretations that may exist before the activity starts.
- Ask for volunteers to lead each breakout room to avoid awkwardness at the start of the discussion or activity.
- If the breakout is meant to produce a tangible result such as a piece of working code or a proposal for an improved way of working, give people time to think about it independently before the breakout. Allotting five minutes for individuals to collect their thoughts helps build confidence and thus more valuable outcomes.
- If hosting a hybrid Dojo, project remote team members on a large screen and point a wide-angled webcam at the group in the room. I strongly recommend not using a

laptop to handle this because the screen is not big enough to see remote participants and the camera does not capture the entire group in one frame.

Try teach-backs. In a teach-back, a team member is responsible for teaching a concept to the rest of the team. This could be a senior developer teaching the group about the tech stack or a Scrum master teaching the group about story splitting. The point is that the Dojo coach is not the only teacher, and people should know their knowledge is valued and feel empowered to share it.

During the teach-back, the Dojo coach is an active participant, asking thought-provoking questions and connecting teachings back to the team's Dojo goals.

People feel deep ownership of a topic when they know that the group depends on them to learn it. As such, teach-backs reinforce learning, help people feel recognized as contributors, and give the team a break from hearing the Dojo coach's voice. All of this drives engagement in the virtual setting. (In any setting, really!)

Inspired by the tomato-shaped kitchen timer, the Pomodoro Technique entails taking short breaks at regular intervals, such as every 25 minutes. You could easily change the length to 30- or 45-minute intervals, but try not to exceed 60-minute intervals.

Pomodoro helps overcome screen fatigue, but more importantly, it keeps participants sharper. Studies show that people tend to operate more efficiently when they return from breaks.

Pomodoro also gives the team an opportunity to bond over a unique team norm. I've shown this technique to multiple teams during the pandemic, and many of those teams have enthusiastically kept it. This is because it goes deeper than stopping work. Pomodoro reminds us to check on each other and prioritizes well-being.

While we're on the topic of well-being, movement is known to improve brain function and boost productivity. John Medina, molecular biologist and author of *Brain Rules*, is a leading expert on optimizing brain function. He claims that even getting up for two to three minutes every half hour to move your joints, roll out your muscles, or go for a quick walk has many benefits such as increasing oxygen flow to your brain and increasing cognition and mental sharpness.

Sometimes people have a hard time moving on their own, so why not make movement a group activity during the virtual Dojo? Walking standups or midday team stretches are great ways to engage the team while getting the blood pumping. The best part is that these activities are accessible and beneficial to almost anyone, in-person or remote.

Technical Coaching Tips for the Virtual Dojo

Whether it is gathering a group of people for a mobbing session around a large screen or sharing a keyboard with another person at a pairing station, common Extreme Programming practices weren't created with social distancing in mind. (Insert nervous laughter.)

The initial solution for attempting to mob or pair in the virtual environment was repurposing the screen-share tooling we already had access to. This worked, but it was hard to keep it engaging because only one person could interact with the code at a time. Let's face it, watching someone else type on a screen is a snooze fest! Especially if you're at home wearing sweatpants. I mean, come on!

I've spent two years in the virtual Dojo setting, and I've found that there are ways we can make programming in the virtual setting something we can stay awake for. Let's explore them.

Instead of a typical screen-sharing tool, try a tool that enables you to collaboratively edit and debug with others in real time, such as Visual Studio Live Share. This capability enables participation for everyone without needing to clone any code repositories or install any dependencies. An added benefit of a real-time collaborative code tool is that developers are able to retain their personal editor preferences, which is a pretty big deal considering that dark themes and light themes have been the center of some interesting debates!

One word: Hackathon! Throw a challenge out there and watch as the team develops mind-blowing solutions. This doesn't have to be too involved. Just carve out a day, form a couple of teams, then meet at the end to pitch ideas and vote for the best one (Table 4.1). Bonus points for working toward implementing the idea in the Dojo. I have yet to host a Hackathon where developers didn't get excited.

Table 4.1. Hackathon Agenda

Opening statements	9:00 a.m.
Review Hackathon expectations, offer Q&A Example: "Ideas must be small enough to be completed in two sprints"	9:10 a.m.
Form teams Note: Splitting a Dojo team into two works well	9:25 a.m.
Present Hackathon challenge Example: "How can we improve the speed of our release cycle?"	9:30 a.m.
Hackathon start	9:45 a.m.
Hackathon end, pitch Hackathon ideas Note: Five minutes per pitch works well	3:30 p.m.
Vote for winning idea Note: The Dojo team votes on the ideas	3:45 p.m.
Crown the winners Example: Winners get announced on broader communication channels like Slack or Teams	3:50 p.m.
Next steps Example: "Commit to writing user stories to bring the idea to life"	3:55 p.m.

The spirit of innovation tends to linger long past the Hackathon and serves as an invigorator for teams.

More Advice for Virtual Dojos

The expression "Out of sight, out of mind" is relevant when we find ourselves not in the same room with each other. A day can pass before you know it, especially if a remote team is spread across time zones.

Nurture excitement and momentum by interacting with the team daily. Interaction does not always have to be a riveting group activity.

It can take the form of a simple gesture such as a poll that sparks some discussion in the team's messaging channel.

Another miscellaneous piece of advice requires things to get awkward. If you ask for participation during the virtual Dojo and all you get is crickets, for the love of God, do not move on. "Getting comfortable with being uncomfortable" is a really powerful sign to teams that you won't let them off the hook for learning. If you just move on without a response, you are signaling that participation is optional in the Dojo. Participation is anything but optional given skill development intent and limited timebox.

Here are some tips for getting people to speak up:

- Let the team know that it can take some time to respond, so you are happy to wait.
- Reframe the question; perhaps it wasn't clear.
- Make the question easier to answer (e.g., a yes/no question).

At any rate, once the team sees that you hold them accountable for participation, the crickets tend to go away. So hang in there, coach!

My last advice for virtual Dojos is to be picky about what you place on team members' calendars.

I'm not sure of the psychology behind this, but when people have crammed calendars, no matter how well intended the meetings are, they become overwhelmed and distracted by the feeling of busyness.

So instead of habitually dropping something on the calendar, try pursuing casual, impromptu discussions instead. You would be surprised how agreeable people are to a spontaneous Zoom or Slack call to chat. What's more, impromptu sessions offer flexibility and allow ideas, challenges, and signals to present themselves organically.

The Future of Virtual Dojos

The most futuristic virtual Dojo I've seen involved 3-D virtual spaces such as Mozilla Hubs. A clever adaptation, indeed, as it takes us beyond a video screen and into a virtual world. However, it still misses the tactility and sensory elements. The same can be said for telepresence technologies.

Although it is in the early innings, the Metaverse brings a substantial immersive dimension to remote work. Imagine walking up to an avatar that resembles your colleague and whiteboarding just as you would in person. You wouldn't be holding the whiteboard marker in your actual hand, but considering the potential of haptic feedback technology, you might be able to feel it in your hand. Perhaps seeing a fully virtual version of your colleague helps to regain the visibility of the invisible group norms that are lost in the remote-work world.

Anyone's guess is fair, but one thing that cannot be refuted is that virtual Dojos are here to stay. Sure, they differ vastly from collocated Dojos, but that does not mean they're inferior. In some ways, virtual Dojos can be the better choice because they make Dojos accessible to distributed teams. There is a benefit to having everyone on the same playing field, removing the mismatch between collocated and remote participation.

The transition to virtual Dojos has been simultaneously scary and rewarding. I wouldn't have succeeded without frequent feedback from the team, creative facilitation, an open mind, and the humility to know things are evolving on the virtual frontier.

An effective Dojo experience is completely possible from the other side of the screen.

5 ■ Making the Case for the Dojo

Companies tend to invest liberally in product development but do not share the same spending enthusiasm when it comes to investing in their people.

Amazon's 2021 annual report shows approximately $50 billion invested in new and existing products.

Statista research tells us that the average spend on learning and development is approximately $1,200 per person. Let's say Amazon pays the $1,200 for all 1 million employees. Even at a staggering $1.2 billion, the projected learning and development cost would only account for 2.4 percent of Amazon's product spend.

This "product over people" disparity seems to be widespread. At Netflix, a $2.3 billion product spend is reflected on the 2021 annual report, where the average learning and development spend would be around $13.5 million. Apple reports $21.9 billion in product spend, where the estimated learning and development cost would be around $44 million.

It is fair to point out that growing people and growing products is not apples to apples. In fact, there are arguably greater costs with developing products. Still, the disparities are so significant it is difficult to rationalize the gap. Less than 5 percent of product spend is expected for growing people.

Why?

Why are companies less willing to invest in learning? Is it because the ROI cannot be easily quantified? Is it because decision makers look at it as more of an optics thing than something that influences the growth of the business? Your guess is as good as mine.

Nonetheless, this chapter aims to address funding challenges head on by exploring techniques that have worked for getting the Dojo funded in real life. We'll cover various approaches and angles that have helped convince leadership why Dojos deserve to be a fixture within the skilling ecosystem of an organization.

In a Nutshell: Grow People to Grow the Business

I've found it is effective to start with the high-level value proposition of the Dojo and then support that with factual stories, studies, and data. With that advice in mind, let's refer to Figure 5.1.

As depicted, we see that the Dojo bridges people—the lifeblood of any business—and real-world practice as a way to establish *sustainable* business growth. Yes, sustainable, as in long lasting,

Figure 5.1: The Dojo Connects People and Real-World Practice to Create Capable People Who Drive Sustainable Business Growth

reliable, maintainable, and practical. Overstated? Exaggerated? Nope. Because we're not talking about the average learning and development ask. This is an investment in people that does not just have the ability to make them, say, a better Java developer. It makes them a better Java developer in the context of a specific business because we're effectively conducting hands-on skill-building while developing domain knowledge. That is a monumental benefit that means people are enabled to contribute to the business sooner by circumventing the timely translation of generic training to real-world application.

Align to Business Outcomes

As with any new investment, the Dojo will need to be aligned to business outcomes to be considered viable to the organization, which means the individuals selling the Dojo must be confident in demonstrating how Dojos influence business outcomes. In other words, what does the Dojo uniquely provide to grow the business? Here are some tips that have helped me to align the Dojo to the organization's business outcomes:

- If your organization has outcomes clearly defined, review and confirm them with leadership from applicable departments (e.g., business, product, technology) to ensure you are aligning to relevant outcomes.
- Investigate the portfolio and program levels of the organization to identify patterns (e.g., innovation, automation) and determine how the Dojo may enable them.
- If you represent a public company, review public announcements such as quarterly shareholder reports to understand priorities that are being communicated outwardly. Check for discrepancies between the shareholder reports and what internal leadership is communicating, because closing this gap is top of mind for leadership and increases your chances of being heard by them.

- For private companies, refer to resources like Crunch-base to see what ideas were pitched to investors to garner funding for the organization. Again, check for discrepancies between the message to investors and the message from internal leadership for the same reason just mentioned.

Sometimes we have to take the initiative and find answers ourselves, or else things may never get done. However, we're not in a vacuum. No matter where you start the Dojo's business alignment process, it is good practice to get agreement from applicable Dojo partners before officially promoting the Dojo (e.g., executive sponsors, business, product, technology).

If this feels like a repeat of the "Approaching the Dojo like a Product" chapter, you're not entirely wrong. When the product canvas is being built out, it is natural to consider the organization's strategic outcomes in the business goals sections (Table 5.1). Pulling from the product canvas is certainly not frowned upon if it sufficiently defines what value currently means to the organization.

Pro tip: as time goes on, the definition of value evolves—meaning the Dojo's alignment with the organization's outcomes is not a one-and-done endeavor. It is critical that the Dojo practice monitor its alignment with the organization and adjust to match the organization's outcomes. Or else the Dojo would be quite literally valueless.

Table 5.1. Dojo Organizational Alignment Example

Strategic outcomes	Dojo skill offerings
Increase time to market by 20%	Value stream optimization, deployment automation
Make our app available on all internet-accessible devices	Responsive design, React Native
Create a more personalized customer experience	Application monitoring and logging, Persona development

The Dojo's Value to the Organization

There are many ways the Dojo can provide significant value back to the wider organization, positioning it for growth on many fronts.

I cannot stress enough how important it is for the Dojo practice to be able to demonstrate the broader impact the Dojo can have across the organization. In my experience, the Dojo is often compartmentalized as an isolated team-level engagement. While that is true in practice, the impact of what is gained in the Dojo stretches much further than a single team.

Let's explore a few compelling ways the Dojo can make an organization—as a whole—better than what it was.

1. The Dojo Supports a Learning Culture and Thus Business Growth

Continuous learning culture was popularized by the DevOps movement that began in the 2010s and has since evolved into a movement in and of itself. Continuous learning culture encompasses a set of values and practices that encourage individuals and the organization as a whole to constantly increase competence, performance, and innovation.

Continuous learning culture is not another fluffy buzzword. The concept has been known to produce real gains back to the business. Learning cultures produce engaged employees who can express their intelligence and creativity, lending the company an important competitive advantage.

Take, for instance, Google. Over the years, Google has become known for its fanatical emphasis on continuous learning. Employees are encouraged to devote a percentage of their time to continuous learning—experimenting, upskilling, and innovating. This learning-first approach has produced breakthrough products such as Gmail, Google Talk, and Google Now, to name a few. It makes you wonder how much of Google's trillion-dollar market cap can be attributed to its continuous learning culture.

Technically, a continuous learning culture can prevail without Dojos. But one can easily see the significant role the Dojo plays in supporting a culture of learning. Dojos provide a place for learning. A place that takes individuals away from the noise of daily routines, so that they can focus purely on learning and growing meaningful skills. By providing the Dojo as a skilling option in an organization, it says, "We have provided a resource to ensure meaningful learning matters to this organization."

2. The Dojo Offers Exceptional Learning Retention

Upskilling is integral to delivering higher-quality products in today's digital-first world. So it is no surprise that organizations spend billions each year on learning and development programs to grow their staff and attempt to narrow ever-widening skill gaps.

Given the relevance and outrageous costs, one might wonder, "From the billions invested, how much of the learning is actually retained?" The truth is that learning development resources are not all the same. There are major differences in levels of effectiveness.

During the 1960s, researcher Edgar Dale theorized that learners retain more information by what they do as opposed to what is heard, read, or observed. He developed a model that incorporates several theories related to instructional design and learning processes, which culminated in the Cone of Experience depicted in Figure 5.2.

Because the Dojo hinges on learning by doing real work, it would fall into the active segment garnering upward of 90 percent retention. This claim correlates well with my experience in the Dojo, too, as I've yet to find a Dojo engagement where learning was not sticky. In fact, on more than one occasion Dojo participants have taken what they've learned from the Dojo further than I imagined, months and years after the Dojo had concluded. The Dojo helped knock over the first domino, so to speak.

Dale helped confirm that learning and development approaches are not the same. How much is your organization spending on passive learning opportunities such as LinkedIn Learning, Pluralsight, and classroom training? Might there be opportunities to adjust strategy toward active, more retentive learning opportunities like the Dojo?

After 2 weeks, we retain…

Reading • 10% of what we READ

Hearing words • 20% of what we HEAR

Seeing • 30% of what we SEE

Watching a demonstration • 50% of what we SEE & HEAR

Discussion Giving a talk • 70% of what we SAY

Dojo → Simulating the real experience Doing the real thing • 90% of what we DO

Figure 5.2: Edgar Dale's Cone of Experience

DOJO STORY: SUPPORTING DALE'S THEORY

One of my first Dojo engagements involved a team that had zero DevOps footprint. They had long talked about getting started on their release automation journey, but like many teams, they couldn't find the time. Dojo goals conversations led us to commit to the ambitious goal of creating a CI/CD pipeline template (adhering to company standards) and using the new template to set up a pipeline for one of their applications so the team would get practice in developing a pipeline template and using it in a real-world application.

We were able to achieve the goal, but that was hardly the impressive part. What was most impressive was that the team went on to develop pipelines for the rest of their applications sans coach and supported other teams within their organization on pipeline efforts.

In the Dojo retrospective, the team attributed their zero-to-hero pipeline transformation to the hands-on coaching style of the Dojo. They were able to build confidence and muscle memory fast by developing the pipeline template with us.

3. The Dojo Creates a Space for Empowered People, So They Make Smarter Decisions

In one Dojo, the team was struggling to find out why reports were showing high user abandonment on a particular form. Digging into call center tickets, we found several tickets related to the form. Callers indicated that they felt caught off-guard by a sudden consent prompt appearing at the very end of the long-form workflow, causing them to abandon the form and reach out to customer support (probably not in the best mood).

The Dojo team was excited to fix this user experience flaw, as it appeared to be a low-effort, high-impact win. You could almost feel the deflation as the technical lead said, "We can't change the order of the consent prompt because it's a compliance requirement. I was told it had to show up at the end of the form."

No one challenged it. They accepted it as reality and moved on as they normally would when they heard the word "compliance."

As Dojo coaches, we pushed the team to take action, which resulted in the team coordinating a meeting with compliance to discuss the issue. Early in the meeting, compliance agreed the prompt would be better at the beginning and they saw no reason for it not to be. The team corrected the order of the prompt, and form abandonment improved right away.

The consent prompt win was not magic. All it took was to empower people to ask questions and suggest a better way. People who feel empowered to ask questions and challenge ideas make smarter decisions. Smarter decisions mean better products, better customer experiences, and, as a result, better business performance.

What if an organization was full of people who were not empowered, people who accepted things because "that's how it has always been"? How many opportunities would be missed because people weren't empowered to seize them? How much cost could have been avoided if people were encouraged to speak up? We will never be able to accurately quantify the true cost of powerless people, but there is enough circumstantial evidence out in the world to state that empowered people create successful organizations.

There are many books on how to empower people (literally anything authored by Brené Brown or David Marquet), so I won't go deep into the topic. The basic recipe for empowerment is providing people with the resources, authority, opportunity, and motivation to do their work, as well as holding them accountable for their actions.

How does the Dojo play a role in empowerment?

The Dojo is driven by experimentation and exploration; therefore, it causes us to ask questions like "What if?" and "Why not?" fueling the fire of empowerment.

4. The Dojo Helps Attract and Retain People

Gallup reports that voluntary turnover costs can range from one-half to two times the employee's annual salary. In other words, if a developer salaried at $100,000 voluntarily leaves your organization, it could cost anywhere from $50,000 to $200,000 to replace them. If you were to multiply that problem by many employees, even *Fortune* 50 organizations would become hindered by numbers like that.

The pain brought on by turnover costs is mind-blowing on its own, but there are other pains that come with it. Turnover diminishes the morale of existing employees because they typically pick up the work of the resigned. The diminished morale can frustrate existing employees to the extent that they leave as well, creating a wildly circular problem.

In evaluating options for deterring turnover, employers instinctively believe employees are resigning because they want to make more money, so they respond with higher compensation or sign-on bonuses. Yet, more compensation doesn't solve the problem. That is because employees value more than money. They want to work for a place that cares about them and values their unique contributions.

Dojos can help employers provide the supportive environment that existing and prospective employees are seeking.

One way the Dojo does this is by responding to the professional development needs of today's employees. Reskilling and upskilling are increasingly important in the job market, with 59 percent of professionals ranking them as a top priority. It is no wonder that, as skill gaps continue to widen due to emerging technologies, employees want to ensure they can remain relevant and productive in their field.

What's more, it seems the priority placed on professional development will be long term, as 76 percent of Gen Z employees see learning as the key to their advancement.

The Dojo also helps alleviate another cause of turnover: lack of meaning.

In the early 2020s, surveys across industries and demographics revealed that feeling disconnected from purpose was the top reason people voluntarily quit their jobs.

If you think about it, the finding makes total sense, especially for highly skilled workers such as developers, engineers, and designers; this worker archetype tends to attach a high level of ownership to their work. This means they take it hard if their work doesn't connect with greater meaning or goes unnoticed.

There is strong psychological evidence supporting a correlation between connectedness to one's work and better mental health. Author Daniel Pink wrote about the concept of intrinsic motivation in his book *Drive*. He explains that it is human nature to become intrinsically motivated when we find our work interesting, challenging, and meaningful. Intrinsically motivated individuals are ultimately happy—in and outside work. This level of deep connectedness in work is known to directly influence an individual's attitude, work performance, and length of tenure.

Dojos are an excellent catalyst for creating intrinsically motivated people. I've witnessed grown adults light up and believe in learning again. Reclusive, seasoned (and probably jaded) developers and engineers getting excited is the type of impact that keeps me coming back to Dojo coaching.

Dojo Value Propositions by Level and Type

Table 5.2 showcases the most influential Dojo value propositions, segmented by organizational level. This format works well because all

Table 5.2. Dojo Value Propositions

Level	Value
Organization	Better products—quality, innovation
	Fosters continuous learning culture
	Talent retention
	Talent attraction
Team	Strengthened psychological safety
	Enhanced cohesiveness—bonding through growth, "one team"
	Cross-training—reduced skill silos
Individual	Renewed morale
	Stronger empowerment
	Recognition—"I can tell the organization cares about me because they invest in my growth"
	Quality learning—long-standing skills that are directly applicable to the individual's role

it takes is a glance to get a sense of the impact the Dojo can bring to an organization.

Dojo Practice Metrics

Up until now, I have not mentioned quantitative measurements related to the Dojo practice, so let's get into that because they are an incredible tool in demonstrating value and keeping the Dojo practice on the right course.

Rather than solely using numbers to demonstrate the value of the Dojo practice, I recommend using them as a means to monitor performance. In other words, if we were to pretend the Dojo practice was a car, the metrics would be the instrument panel right behind the steering wheel. Are we going too slow? Too fast? Is the engine temperature okay? This real-time data helps us make decisions that affect outcomes.

Sticking with the car analogy, it's crucial that the instrument panel gives us the data that matters. So when you define which metrics will be used for monitoring the effectiveness of the Dojo practice, you will want to derive the metrics from strategy. A good artifact for this is the business goals section of the Product Vision Board featured in Chapter 3 (Figure 5.3).

The sample business goal reads, "The Dojo responds to the organization's modernization goals by equipping people to effectively develop products in today's digital-first world." Let's pretend we used the Dojo practice's business goal as a communication tool to align with key people around the organization on what the Dojo practice metrics should be.

- Because our modernization efforts include increasing speed to market, we opt to use a team's cycle time as a standard Dojo practice metric. *Goal: Equal to or less than two weeks.*
- We also select the team-level microservices competency because we are interested in skilling people in decoupling monolithic applications. *Goal: Competency score equal to or greater than 2 (source: skills matrices).*
- Lastly, we land on the customer net promoter score to ensure product quality is maintained while we grow as an organization. *Goal: Equal to or greater than an 8.*

Here is what that Dojo Practice Dashboard could look like at Pre-Dojo and Post-Dojo (Figure 5.4 and Figure 5.5). With this data, we can determine if the Dojo practice is supporting business goals.

Take note to evaluate Dojo practice metrics (or the instrument panel) regularly to ensure they are helping to tell the right story; at

VISION — What is your motivation for creating the product? Which positive change should it bring about?

Develop people in Agile, DevOps, and XP programming to enhance the capabilities of the broader organization.

 TARGET GROUP

Which market or market segment does the product address?

Who are the target customers and users?

Developers and engineers looking to develop their technical skills

Scrum masters looking to hone their coaching skills to enable higher-performing teams

Product owners looking to hone their product-thinking skills to create powerful value for the organization

 NEEDS

What problem does the product solve?

Which benefit does it provide?

The Dojo aims to narrow the ever-widening skill gaps in technology and products that hinder the organization from meeting strategic objectives.

Additionally, professional development helps reduce turnover because people feel their learning journeys are valued.

 PRODUCT

What product is it?

What makes it stand out?

Is it feasible to develop the product?

The Dojo is effective in addressing needs because it supports long-lasting skill development.

A notable differentiator for Dojos is that they involve building skills while delivering on work.

BUSINESS GOALS

How is the product going to benefit the company?

What are the business goals?

The Dojo responds to the organization's modernization goals by equipping people to effectively develop products in today's digital-first world.

Figure 5.3: Example Product Vision Board

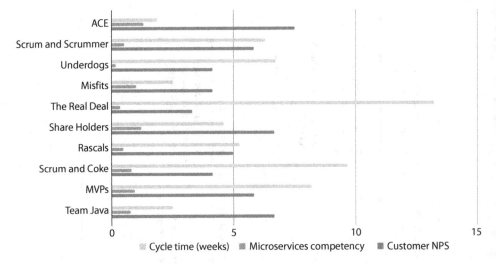

Figure 5.4: Dojo Practice Dashboard: Pre-Dojo Results

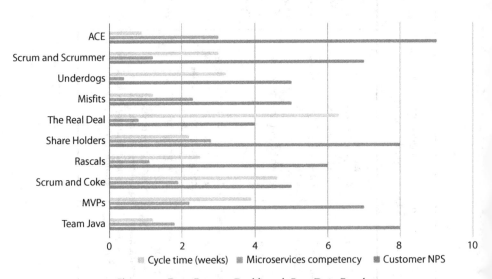

Figure 5.5: Dojo Practice Dashboard: Post-Dojo Results

the very least every quarter. Business strategy is evolving, and so should the ways we measure it.

Simplified Example of a Cost-Benefit Analysis

Since we are neck-deep in justifying the investment of a Dojo practice, I figured now would be a good time to consider a very, very simplified cost-benefit analysis (Table 5.3). The intent is to give you a realistic idea of how to present the financials of a Dojo practice.

You could add several more benefits to the list to justify your spend, but even with the two real-world examples I've added, we can clearly see that it doesn't take much to demonstrate that the Dojo pays for itself and then some.

Pilots Are Powerful

I am unabashedly from the "Show Me State," which lines up well with the method of proving one's claims. No matter how organized your pitch is, most times the best way to convince people of something is to show them.

If you find yourself lacking momentum or if you are concerned it will be hard to sell the Dojo in your organization, propose a pilot Dojo.

This is a low-cost, low-risk way to validate fit. Some leaders have been burned by things looking great on paper but turning out to be impractical in the organization's environment, so trepidation is common and understandable.

Advice on How to Approach the Dojo Pitch

I don't have experience pitching on *Shark Tank* or securing series A, B, or C funding. But I have successfully pitched the Dojo at multiple organizations. Here are a few tips that could help you seal the deal.

Table 5.3. Annualized Cost-Benefit Analysis for Dojo Practice

Costs		
Need	**Cost**	**Rationale**
Four Dojo coaches (total compensation, benefits)	$800,000	Individuals who are skilled in immersive learning to maximize Dojo impact
Professional development for Dojo coaches	$40,000	To keep Dojo coaches sharp on emerging Agile, product, and technology trends in order to maintain coaching quality
Remote-work tooling	N/A	Covered by shared services budget
Incidentals	$10,000	Office supplies, happy hours, promotional materials
Benefits		
Targets	**Calculations**	**Results**
10% reduction in employee turnover (Agile-, product-, and technology-related groups)	$50,000 recruitment costs × 300 employees × 0.10	$1.5 million savings
10% fewer production defects	$1.1 million (annualized cost of defects) × 0.10	$110,000 savings + company reputation preservation
	$1.6 million (total benefits) − $850,000 (total costs)	
Total costs = +$750,000		

1. Know Your Must-Make Points

To successfully sell your Dojo, you must familiarize yourself with the goals and values of the decision makers. In their article "Get the Boss to Buy In," Susan Ashford and James Detert tell us that senior leaders who "don't already perceive an idea's relevance to organizational performance don't deem it important enough to merit their attention." That means you have to consider the Dojo from their perspective and make it relevant to their needs. Why should they listen to you? What's in it for them? What do you want them to do about it? The answers to these questions should be clear before you present them to leadership.

2. Bring Your Must-Make Points to Life

Show your boss how the Dojo is both relevant and valuable. Connect it to something that is already familiar and real by painting a vivid picture or telling a compelling story that resonates with decision makers. This will increase the likelihood that they'll be able to connect dots and become personally invested in the Dojo's success and, in turn, rally others to become powerful advocates.

To help transform your must-make points into compelling narratives, ask these questions:

- How is the Dojo relevant to organizational priorities?
- How can I connect the Dojo to issues that are already receiving attention?
- How can I emphasize the opportunities the Dojo creates for the organization?

3. Be Mindful of Your Timing

"Timing is everything" is not a cliché, it's everything. Timing can make the difference between your Dojo taking off and its being shelved.

Finding the perfect moment to introduce the Dojo isn't an exact science, but you can learn to identify the ideal time when it arises. Start by being sensitive to changes in your organization such as leadership changes, other new ideas that are being introduced, or external market trends that are emerging that might influence internal operations. Asking these questions can also help:

- How and when are decisions usually made in my organization (e.g., annual budgeting)?
- What's happening outside the organization, and will it distract from leaders seeing the value of the Dojo?

4. Create Partnerships

Performance is not measured by the ideas you bring to the table, but rather by what is accomplished for the organization. You must be able to transform the Dojo into results, and that can't happen if you're working alone. You need the cooperation and support of others. You need partners.

Partners are advocates who fully understand the value of the Dojo and want to see it succeed. More importantly, these allies will work alongside you to help champion the Dojo in various ways, from providing valuable insight and expertise to protecting you from performance killers (i.e., the people who are most likely to block your progress).

Ask these questions to identify partnerships:

- Who in my network can help me sell the Dojo up?
- How might I strategically involve them?
- Who are my potential performance killers and fence-sitters?

6 ■ Marketing the Dojo

What good is a Dojo if no one knows about it? Getting the word out seems like an obvious step, right?

Even the most effective and proven Dojo practices can benefit from public relations to help keep them staffed and funded and to ensure demand for a healthy backlog of potential teams.

This chapter covers methods I've seen work well for effectively sharing the Dojo story so that your organization has a strong understanding of the Dojo's purpose, benefits, and potential.

Know Your Audience

Before you start getting the word out, having an understanding of who should be receiving your message is crucial.

Generally, there are two core audiences for the Dojo:

- prospective Dojo teams
- leadership that has an influence on prospective Dojo teams

Prospective Dojo teams as a core audience is a no-brainer because without them we wouldn't have people to coach in the Dojo. Messaging that may appeal to Dojo teams includes the following:

- "Learn by doing."
- "Be ready for next-generation technology."
- "Upskill using your team's backlog."

I discussed how leadership's support for Dojo teams is paramount in "The Role of Leaders in the Dojo" in Chapter 2. A quick recap: the team's leadership must be bought in to green-light the Dojo, and they must commit to making space for learning, which are necessary ingredients for success. For these reasons, they are a core audience. Consider messaging that appeals to leadership:

- "Teams learn new techniques by delivering against their backlog."
- "Squash skill silos."
- "Better skills mean better products."

Once you've determined your core audiences, try using an empathy map (Figure 6.1) to help shed light on whom you're talking to,

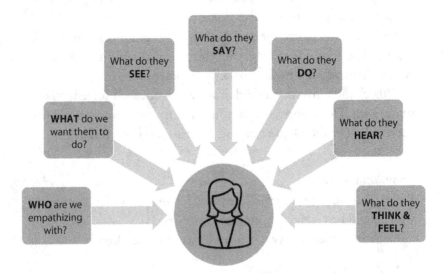

Figure 6.1: Empathy Map

what they care about, and what influences them. These insights are incredibly powerful in how you approach your Dojo messaging.

Meet Them Where They Are

Daniel Priestley, in his book *Oversubscribed: How to Get People Lining Up to Do Business with You*, examines the phenomenon in which businesses don't chase clients but rather clients chase them. This is an especially impressive feat because we live in a world of endless choices.

One of the sections in Priestley's book gets into why meeting customers where they're at helps with creating insatiable demand. He writes, "You are in the business of transformation: moving people from their current state to something they want even more. If you want to take people on a journey, you must meet them where they are, communicate with them in the language that resonates with them now and show them a clear picture of where they will end up if they go with you."

This line of thinking works fantastically well with the Dojo. As a Dojo coach, you encounter organizations and teams with different challenges, complexities, and backgrounds. While there is no one-size-fits-all way to overcome each Dojo's challenges, the approach of meeting teams where they are is the only real way to connect with Dojo prospects.

Often, meeting them where they are requires effort. An effort is made to patiently guide Dojo prospects as they peel back each layer to reveal what a Dojo may mean for them. An effort is made to get ahead of any trepidation and alleviate it with substantive reasoning. An effort is made toward creating a crystal ball that shows candidates what could specifically materialize if they pursue a Dojo engagement.

All of these efforts can be draining, but when you see the light switch on and a new Dojo ambassador being born right before your eyes, it is completely worth it.

Build a Fan Club of Leaders

Leaders motivate us to go places that we would never otherwise go. They are needed both to change organizations and to produce results. In many business climates, good leadership is revered as the most important competitive advantage a company can have. Given this, it is not surprising that when respected leaders communicate a message, not only do people listen, they typically feel compelled to agree.

So my advice is to leverage leadership's power of influence. Converting respected leaders into fans of the Dojo is a powerful way to generate lasting exposure and interest across the organization.

For example, in a past role, my colleagues and I were lucky enough to get the attention of the chief technology officer. No, it wasn't as if we got a meeting with him and we were able to convince him that the Dojo was the bee's knees right then and there. We wish it were that easy! Instead, we took the path of persistence. We never missed a chance to share Dojo stories at department meetings or in company communications. We would talk to anyone who was even remotely interested in Dojos. When we received feedback from Dojo teams, we would unabashedly ask them to email it to us because this would allow us to forward the success up the hierarchical chain. We made the Dojo impossible to ignore.

Eventually, we started noticing the CTO, of all people, mentioning the Dojo to his direct reports, to his peers, and in a few communications. We were equally surprised and humbled. We took his outward endorsement of the Dojo as an invitation to reach out to him, and that ultimately became the springboard for a fruitful executive sponsorship.

I am not saying that creating a fan club of leaders is easy—it is quite the opposite. It may take several months or years, and the truth is you may never reach the executive level. But time is rarely wasted when you put it into forging relationships with people in the position of influence. It can make the difference in the growth trajectory of the Dojo.

Where to Share the Dojo

In real estate they say "location, location, location" to embody the idea that no matter how nice a property may be, its location largely determines its value. The same theory can be applied to advertising in that you could have a remarkable message, but if it's being shared in a location with little to no visibility, the advertisement becomes moot.

Where you choose to share your Dojo is about as important as whether you choose to share the Dojo.

Where you share the Dojo reflects back on the Dojo's reputation. If people see the Dojo on the agenda at a department meeting or in other high-profile settings, it builds legitimacy. It says someone in the position of influence sees potential in the Dojo, or else they wouldn't be allocating time to it.

Great. So where exactly should we share the Dojo? Let's get into specific suggestions.

Earlier, I suggested that leveraging leadership's influence can be powerful in getting the word out about the Dojo. What if we were able to access multiple leaders at once, maximizing the chances of leadership endorsement? You can do this by getting the Dojo added to a leadership meeting agenda.

Leadership meetings consist of senior leadership or a management team organizing and taking part in a recurring meeting, typically once a week, where important information is shared that is needed to make key decisions about the business. This is a meeting where decisions are made, problems are solved, and the leadership team discusses important issues such as operations, key metrics, and future business.

Leadership meetings teem with passion for growing the organization. Everyone in the room is interested in learning about thought-provoking ideas that can demonstrate tangible value back to the organization (ahem . . . like the Dojo). Chances are, the leaders in the room already have a positivity bias toward the Dojo because of what it intrinsically offers (e.g., innovation, improved skilling, empowered people), and all you need to do is drive it home.

Another great place to share the Dojo is at large-format meetings such as department- or organization-wide meetings. I can support that with a true story: I know a coach who received 50-some Dojo inquiries immediately following his presentation at a department meeting.

I like large-format meetings because they are an efficient way to get in front of different types of audiences in one fell swoop. This can support the Dojo on multiple fronts—leadership support, candidate team interest, and Dojo coach recruiting.

In large-format meetings, the Dojo can unify people across roles and departments because it brings value that everyone cares about—everyone recognizes that skill development is crucial to the organization's success. This unity gives people a reason to talk to each other, and that chatter builds momentum for the Dojo.

Similarly, center of excellence or center of practice groups related to product, Agile, or tech are also great spots to share the Dojo. They, too, can be large format, but they usually attract an audience of specialized practitioners, which presents unique opportunities.

For one, specialized practitioners have an in with prospective Dojo teams. They are familiar with challenges that occur at the team level and bring those insights to the table. This is useful for tailoring Dojo communications and offerings.

The other thing is that if the Dojo passes the practitioners' sniff test, the practitioners are more than likely to spread the good word. This means that the respect you gain from the practitioners weighs a lot and can significantly affect the Dojo's street cred.

Don't feel limited to piggybacking off of existing meetings in your organization. I have had success in setting up brand-new sessions exclusively for the Dojo. See if you can get access to distribution lists for sending invites to Agile teams by checking with a CoE/CoP lead, administrative assistant, or communications coordinator.

A theme with all of the suggestions for promoting the Dojo is that they require asking for help from people outside the Dojo. Don't let this deter you. More times than not, people want to help. So just ask!

Digital Communications

People who work in technology and product spend most of their time working on a screen, so digital communications are a must for advertising the Dojo.

It is a good idea to make friends with the people in internal corporate communications. They can help you spread the word on various high-profile internal platforms.

- Emails—newsletters, memos, messaging on behalf of leadership
- Intranet—banners, articles, interviews
- Internal social networks—Slack, Teams, Yammer
- Internal audio and visual—video interviews, podcast interviews

Internal communication is powerful in its own right, but getting exposure for the Dojo externally can be game-changing. The Dojo at Target (dojo.target.com) is an excellent example of that. It is a publicly accessible website that showcases the Dojo within the Target organization. While the Dojo at Target does not serve teams outside Target, this website helps to build a broader community around the Dojo, which invites external feedback to grow the Dojo at Target, as well as attracting potential hires for Dojo coach roles and technical, product, and Agile roles. Additionally, external credibility develops internal interest. If your organization will permit an external website for your Dojo, I highly recommend you prioritize building it.

And who knows? The external Dojo website could be a catalyst for partnering with the folks in external corporate communications to align the Dojo's story with the broader organization. Now that would be cool!

Regardless of whether you have an external Dojo website or not, it is good practice to have an internal Dojo website so the internal teams the Dojo serves have a place to land for learning about Dojo offerings and Dojo coaches and inquiring about the Dojo.

Make It Share-Worthy

A major way to improve digital communications—websites, videos, documents, decks, and so on—is to make sure the content is shareable. And when I say shareable, I don't mean just technically shareable; I also mean content that people feel compelled to share.

A study conducted by UCLA psychologists found that people have an intrinsic desire to share information and remain aware of how the things they are seeing will be useful not only to themselves but also to others. Content that makes readers feel connected or evokes thought and emotion often makes them want to inform and include others. If a topic resonates with us, we think others will appreciate it too.

An excellent way to provide share-worthy content is by storytelling. Storytelling is a fundamental human activity that unites people and drives stronger, deeper connections. From the earliest recorded history, storytelling has been used as a primary method for human beings to communicate, educate, share, and connect.

Storytelling for the Dojo can mean hearing about the experience from the Dojo coaches. But in my experience, hearing about the Dojo from former Dojo participants generates high-quality content that resonates incredibly well with people.

I've interviewed product owners, Scrum masters, developers, and leaders who engaged in a Dojo. While the interviews were unscripted, they organically produced golden quotes that compelled people to share and talk about the Dojo.

The interview does not need to be a Hollywood production or require special skills. I've done written interviews over email and I've interviewed participants through Zoom and shared the recorded video without much editing. If you can get the participants talking, it will produce content that people connect with.

Consistency Is Key

It can be difficult to keep the broader Dojo conversation alive when you are also preparing teams for the Dojo. The most effective way to continue to fan the flame on the Dojo's relevance is to establish a cadence for getting fresh content out.

Table 6.1. Example Content Calendar

May		
Day	Content/event	Reasoning
May 3	Executive memo: Jane's announcement	Announce new Dojo coach
May 15	Blog: Practical TDD tips from a Dojo coach	Promote test-driven development
May 29	All-hands meeting: ACE team Dojo experience	Storytelling opportunity

A traditional content calendar works well for keeping the Dojo practice accountable to marketing. Table 6.1 provides a basic version of a content calendar demonstrating how easy it can be.

You'll notice from the example that the Dojo does not need to be a content powerhouse. A few plugs a month is usually adequate to nurture relevance.

The other benefit of maintaining a content calendar is that it eliminates the overhead that comes with scrambling around to figure out what to put out next. A content calendar can save you from headaches and help reserve energy for meaningful endeavors like sharpening your Dojo coaching.

Get Scrappy

In a lot of ways, launching your Dojo is a lot like launching a startup because in both cases you are usually establishing your reputation and generating demand from nothing.

One particular instance comes to mind where a bit of scrappiness helped my Dojo development efforts. I was struggling with how to describe the Dojo to prospects. I was able to pitch the concept well, but getting a prospect to understand the day-to-day flow or imagine how being in a Dojo might feel was a challenge for me. Because I believed in the Dojo, I was confident that if I could get prospects to connect more deeply, they would be more likely to pursue it. So I threw on my scrappy hat and asked, "What better way to convey the Dojo than letting someone see a Dojo in real time?" With the Dojo team's permission, I invited prospects such as heads of product or heads of engineering to Dojo sessions. I also invited teams related to the Dojo team because they were familiar with the team's context, which meant they would appreciate the team's growth more. Sensitive sessions such as retrospectives were off-limits to visitors, but sessions that were suitable for transparency (e.g., backlog management) provided the potential for guests to become involved.

Being scrappy can be draining because your wheels are constantly turning. Still, it is incredibly rewarding when you see the seeds you planted in the Dojo's network start to grow and cross-pollinate to create opportunities.

7 ■ Don't Be That Dojo Coach

If you find yourself in a role that directly influences and shapes people (e.g., Dojo coaching), you'd be the world's biggest hypocrite if you didn't work on yourself.

Dojos demonstrate that habits and behaviors can improve through accountability, humility, and practice. In this chapter, we'll hold true to that sentiment by calling out Dojo coach antipatterns so we avoid becoming "that Dojo coach."

Don't Talk Too Much

We've made it to slide 37 about user story splitting. For the last hour, the only voice heard has been the Dojo coach's. Wait—was that a yawn? Probably.

Brevity is crucial because it supports emphasizing hands-on practice as the primary form of teaching in the Dojo. Sharon Bowman, author of *Training from the Back of the Room!*, states, "As long as learners are passively sitting and listening to us talk, they are not learning much," and that statement aligns well with the Dojo. Habits and muscle memory come from an individual's participation in hands-on practice, not listening to a Dojo coach going on a long spiel.

I thus recommend that lectures and presentations do not consume more than 25 percent of the Dojo engagement. Challenge yourself as a coach to keep this number as low as possible.

Don't Be Too Soft

Many Dojo coaches come from coaching engagements where the breadth is massive (e.g., Agile transformation) and the expectation is that it will take several months or years to begin seeing the impact. This type of pace tends to allow coaches to become passive.

Because we have just six weeks to make a meaningful impact, the Dojo demands assertiveness and decisiveness from coaches.

This means going toe-to-toe with challenges without preparation. Getting the team to move beyond their comfort zone right out of the gate. Stomaching awkward moments where the team becomes eerily quiet as they mentally process the rapid growth and general newness. Taking risks by opening up cans of worms and not having the luxury of time to craft a scholarly answer.

This shooting-from-the-hip, hyperaccelerated form of coaching is not meant for all coaches. Generally, coaches with a decade or more of field experience have the empirical knowledge and confidence to coach in this way. But a decade's worth of experience isn't always needed. I've witnessed people who were once team managers or developers become great Dojo coaches. As long as you lead with empathy, remain coachable, and are hell-bent on connecting learning and delivery, you can coach a Dojo.

Don't Suggest That the Dojo Is Transformative to an Organization

Dojos are not intended to transform organizations.

Dojos will not radically improve the organization's market position or provide a competitive advantage. Ouch. It hurts when you read it, doesn't it?

Even if every team inside an organization went through a Dojo, the organizational challenges (adopting agility, company culture, technical and Agile practices, and every other challenge that existed before the Dojo) may prevail.

The fact is, Dojos transform teams. The intent of the Dojo hinges on meeting a team where they are at to bridge any gaps they may have in order to best support the organization. This learning-based approach produces outcomes such as improved product quality, better technical excellence, and experiential learning, which are all long-term, sustainable benefits back to the organization. Still, Dojos are supportive to the organization, not transformative.

If we misrepresent the Dojo as something it is not, then we set the wrong expectations. If expectations are not met, then that could damage the Dojo practice's reputation or cause the people with the purse strings to reevaluate the Dojo entirely.

Don't Become a Snitch for Leadership

Consider the model of the Dojo: a Dojo coach enters a team to work directly on the unique challenge areas of a team. The model itself integrates the Dojo coach deeply into the team as a counselor and beacon of hope. Naturally, the Dojo coach spends hours and hours with the team and individuals of the team, often discussing sensitive topics such as team dynamics. Think of it like this: the Dojo coach gets to see what goes on behind closed doors, and they need to do this so that they can coach effectively. The vulnerability that comes with inviting the Dojo coach behind closed doors means the team places an immense amount of trust in them. I cannot express enough how incredibly special this trust is. As a coach, you should do everything possible to protect it.

Attempting to institute some type of surveillance, leaders in the Dojo team's organization have been known to press the Dojo coach for information about individual and team behavior. If the Dojo coach is not careful with what information is shared with the leadership, it can be used to take action on the team, which destroys any trust that has been created in the Dojo. When trust is broken, it's

Table 6.2. Snitch versus Not a Snitch

Snitch	Not a snitch
"Matt feels that Susan is a terrible Scrum master and refuses to take her seriously."	"A core issue is that the team has different interpretations of their roles."
"Jack says he will leave the company if we move forward with the migration to AWS."	"Some members of the team do not speak up because they feel it doesn't do any good."

game over; it's unlikely that you will get the trust back and be able to connect with the team again.

Earlier in the book, I explained why it is critical that the Dojo coach interfaces with leaders to prepare them for supporting the team during and after the Dojo. So the key question is what to share so you don't become a snitch. I advise keeping team information on a need-to-know basis; however, if it is something that is worthwhile for a leader to know, speak in generalities and leverage knowledge that is openly available (Table 6.2).

If a leader does try to exploit your position as a Dojo coach, hold your ground. Even better, turn it into a coaching moment for the leader.

Don't Get Distracted

Things get exciting and energetic in the Dojo, and it is easy to geek out. In fact, as you proceed along the Dojo Roadmap, you will reveal more and more improvement areas for the team that are just begging to be addressed. But if we stopped and acted on every area of improvement, we would risk not having any tangible gains by the end of the Dojo.

As a Dojo coach, you must keep the Dojo laser-focused on Dojo goals. You are here for a good time, not a long time. Six weeks goes by faster than you think.

Take note of the improvement areas that exist outside the Dojo goals; we certainly don't want to turn a blind eye to them. I've found these notes are great for the team's awareness and as candidates for future Dojo goals.

Don't Sleep on Enablement Teams (e.g., DevOps, Infrastructure, Security, Data)

Around winter 2020, I was sitting in a conference room with the platform team at work. The team was interested in a Dojo, so I was going through my usual speaking points.

Then, out of nowhere, it hit me: the platform team's challenges are inherently the challenges of every application team they support. If we could help optimize the platform team, that could mean enabling more frequent deployments, better logging and monitoring, and faster commitment to deploy lead time.

Obviously, it was a no-brainer to move forward with the platform team Dojo, and as it turned out, our hypothesis of "filling many needs with one deed" was spot on.

Faster requests to provision lead time and improved deployment autonomy created instantaneous benefits across application teams, which in turn created an abundance of Dojo interest among the application teams. We weren't mad at that!

My actionable advice here is to add criteria on your Dojo scoring guide that are preferential to enablement teams. You'll be glad you did.

Don't Do a Dojo with a Team That Won't Remain a Team

This is one of those things that has caused real pain for me as a Dojo coach. Oh, goodness. Here we go.

You might meet a team that seems like the perfect Dojo team. Everyone is enthusiastic about learning, there appear to be clear ways the Dojo could help them, and their leadership has made space for them to grow. You consult your Dojo scoring and it appears this team scores the highest in the backlog, too. Everything falls into place and the Dojo starts off strong. The team's growth mindset is excellent, just as you expected.

In week 4, right as the team begins getting comfortable with practicing without much Dojo coach involvement, a sudden announcement decimates the value of your perfect Dojo.

The announcement informs everyone that a reorganization will be taking place in the coming weeks that will effectively break up the dream team that is currently engaged in the Dojo.

Sure, all is not lost, as some learnings will carry on with individuals, but since the Dojo is catered to this specific team, most of the learnings may not be carried on. The Dojo is exceptionally retentive, and a big reason why is that the coaching is tailored to the team's idiosyncrasies and environment. If you remove the idiosyncrasies and environment, the retention is not as strong.

No one has a crystal ball to be able to predict when reorganizations will happen, so the best way to prevent the disbandment of a Dojo team is to investigate the likelihood of a reorganization as part of the intake phase.

Don't Forget to Consult with Fellow Dojo Coaches

The Dojo coaching community (internal or external to your Dojo practice) is very supportive. Don't forget that.

Countless times, I have used the "phone a friend" method to get advice from fellow Dojo coaches while in the midst of a Dojo. It has been valuable in revealing blind spots.

For instance, a while back I was chatting with a fellow Dojo coach about a Dojo engagement that I was involved in. I went on casually sharing details about the engagement, Dojo goals, and tech stack. I also shared that I found the team's openness about sharing compliments and building each other up to be a particularly special attribute.

Out of nowhere, the fellow coach challenged me to investigate the team's surplus of compliments because it reminded him of Kim Scott's ideals on ruinous empathy in her book *Radical Candor*. Ruinous empathy is when praise isn't specific enough to be helpful or it is criticism that is too nice and unclear.

The truth is I got too close to the team to notice that constructive feedback or disagreement was nonexistent for them. And while a conflict-free environment may seem like a utopia, it presents a major risk to the team's growth because conflict allows the team to synthesize diverse perspectives and ensure solutions, decisions, and ideas are well thought out.

Bottom line: the coach's outside perspective helped reveal a serious issue with psychological safety on the team and his insights changed the entire course of the Dojo.

That was one of many times where I walked away better after confiding in a fellow Dojo coach. That is why, when I am engaged in a Dojo, I try to meet daily with the other Dojo coaches in my organization's Dojo practice for advice, trading notes, or a gut check with another person who understands the complexities of Dojo coaching.

Don't Miss Breaks from the Dojo

For six weeks, a Dojo coach is dedicated to developing a team of people to make progress toward goals that are intentionally meaningful and dear to the team and, inherently, the organization. These goals are localized to the team, so there is no playbook, framework, training class, or Googling that can provide the solution to achieving the team's goal or help prepare the Dojo coach in any way.

In order to connect with the individuals so the coaching is influential, the Dojo coach spends time creating a relationship with each member of the team. This may be one-on-ones, lunch, or happy hour to ensure the foundations of trust are established.

In no time, the Dojo coach becomes part of the team, attending their meetings and interacting with them on a full-time basis, and it's that level of high-touch involvement that makes Dojo coaching so effective.

It is for these reasons I set a clear expectation that I am 100 percent dedicated to the Dojo when I am in a coaching engagement. There isn't much time or brain capacity for other intellectual work.

All said, the side-effect of Dojo coaching is that it can seriously wear you out. Some days you feel drained, your brain is mush from being "on" all day, and your voice is gone. My wife calls this "too much peopling."

Dojo coaching takes work. A lot of work. But it is rewarding and worthwhile work. The rapid gains and team connectedness make the long days not so bad.

Still, the intensity of the Dojo coaching will cause just about anyone to be burned out. So it is absolutely critical that you take breaks from Dojo coaching.

My recommendation is that you take a break from Dojo coaching for two to four weeks following each Dojo engagement to replenish your energy, pursue your own professional development, and develop the Dojo practice as a product.

Dojos are in demand, as indicated by the dozens of Dojo coach job postings currently on Indeed. But Dojos can't exist without Dojo coaches, so please take care of yourself so you can continue your great work in building others.

In All Seriousness

This chapter is more than face-palming and eye-rolling about Dojo coach antipatterns. It is an attempt to spread awareness about the significant impact a person can have on other people. Especially for those in the position of shaping others: teachers, counselors, parents, and coaches of all kinds. These individuals possess a level of influence so great that their shortcomings can result in long-term consequences for other human beings. When you decide to pursue a role such as Dojo coaching, you are also committing to ongoing self-awareness and endless evolution of yourself so that you are creating a desirable impact.

Here are behaviors and outcomes to strive for:

- You embrace empathy, meet people where they are at, and offer relevant advice that best fits people's unique situations. Generally, you ascribe to the "interested inquirer" mindset, asking lots of questions without the air of judgment.
- You practice true active listening in that you do more listening than talking, make good eye contact, and

physically point your body toward the person you're listening to (even over a webcam).

- You are so dedicated and focused that the team feels like they're your only team.
- You are so obsessed with the team's progression toward their goals, you celebrate them without mentioning your own personal impact.
- A feeling of relief fills the air when your name is mentioned or you come into the room.

Conclusion

One of my favorite quotes is by Confucius. It goes like this: "I hear and I forget. I see and I remember. I do and I understand." Every time I read the quote, I crack a smile because it's as if the quote was created specifically for the Dojo. I am humbled to know that the individual credited with establishing the art of teaching over 2,000 years ago believed that doing is the key to true understanding.

While Dojo coaching is synonymous with "learning by doing," there is significant benefit in getting advice before the *doing* from experienced Dojo coaches on areas such as developing a Dojo practice, implementing a proven roadmap for operating a Dojo engagement, selling the idea of a Dojo to an organization, and identifying Dojo coach antipatterns so that you can hone effectiveness early. Especially if the advice has been compiled and packaged up in a nice little pocket guide for you. (See what I did there?)

In today's climate of the Great Resignation where employees are leaving organizations in droves and rapidly emerging technology demands constant skill development, the Dojo is becoming increasingly relevant and urgent. Considering the clear urgency, this book is meant to help you navigate Dojo coaching with more confidence so that you can respond to the growing needs of individuals and organizations in a timely and effective manner.

The truth is, there is no body of writing or resource that can transform a person into a Dojo coach.

So my recommended action for you—an aspiring or experienced Dojo coach—is to go get immersed in a Dojo as soon as possible. Observe a Dojo, become a second coach in a Dojo, or even serve as a guest facilitator for a one-off session. Go find experienced Dojo coaches and get to know them, develop relationships with them, and open the door to learning, mentorship, and collaboration.

If you hadn't noticed yet, my ultimate advice to you for becoming a better Dojo coach is to (ironically) learn by doing. The best way to get better in such a complex and unpredictable space is to develop the muscle memory and bank of empirical experience that keeps your coaching acuity strong.

I was once asked the impossible question, "Jess, what is your least favorite thing about the Dojo?" The answer came to me in an instant.

My least favorite thing about the Dojo is closing a Dojo engagement.

Sure, goodbyes are not always forever, but you become so embedded into the team that it turns into a bittersweet thing.

Unlike this book, the team's Dojo journey is never-ending, as the Dojo learnings and mindsets open up worlds of possibilities.

So, Dojo coach, what worlds will you help open?

What is the difference between Agile coaching, technical coaching, and Dojo coaching?

Agile coaching is intended to help organizations, teams, and individuals adopt Agile practices and methods while embedding Agile values and mindsets.

Agile is easy to understand but hard to master, resulting in many organizations running into problems when taking the leap. Most of these problems come about due to unrealistic expectations of how easy it is to implement Agile within a team, a department, or the whole organization.

Agile coaching seeks to figure out the reasons why Agile is not delivering the expected outcomes and what steps need to be taken to optimize agility, value delivery, and flow for the organization as a whole.

The key takeaway is that Agile coaching leans toward optimization and driving Agile adoption so that organizations can get and stay on the right track for agility.

Technical coaching involves coaching technical practices in an Agile environment. This could take the form of driving the adoption of both Extreme Programming and continuous delivery practices that add value to the development process, selecting and implementing appropriate technology and tools that support Agile ways of working, maintaining a sound architectural foundation that supports business agility, and identifying technical debt and making its impact transparent to the business.

Technical coaching takes a hands-on approach by leading by example in problem-solving and taking care to explain the thought process used when resolving technical issues.

Dojo coaching develops a team's skills and behaviors in a wide range of Agile and technical areas that make up their T-shaped skills. In essence, Dojo coaches are a blend of Agile and technical coaches. Some Dojo coaches have specialties such as technical expertise or executive coaching. In any case, all Dojo coaches have the ability to coach across a spectrum because they need to confidently adapt to provide meaningful coaching in real time.

In addition to having the ability to coach in many areas, the key differentiator in Dojo coaches is the notion of coaching for learning.

Coaching for learning seeks to develop skills and behaviors first, whereas coaching for delivery is placed second.

Refer to the section called "Dojo: Maximizing Effectiveness" in Chapter 2 for more specific Dojo coaching examples.

How many Dojo coaches should be in a Dojo?

Short answer: one to two. I prefer two.

I have coached successful Dojos completely on my own. I have also partnered with another Dojo coach for multiple Dojos and they were successful.

The main reason I coached Dojos solo was the unavailability of Dojo coaches. It was purely out of necessity, not out of preference. I've never coached a Dojo with two coaches and thought, "I wish this was just me." That's because there is so much value in having two Dojo coaches.

And that's because it is incredibly valuable to have another coach's perspective about the team.

For one, if you are able to pair two Dojo coaches who complement each other (e.g., one is more technical, one is more Agile), it provides a more well-rounded, higher-quality coaching experience.

A second reason is that it is so lovely to have another coach you can collaborate with, brainstorm with, and confide in when you are involved in a Dojo engagement. My Dojo coach counterparts have provided many gut checks and pieces of advice.

Third, it's nice for the team to get a break from working with the same person. In fact, some people may be more open to sharing with one Dojo coach over the other. It could be a matter of personality types or shared interests, but that openness supports a more meaningful engagement.

So why stop at two coaches? I cannot say that I've tried a Dojo with more than two coaches, but I suspect it would create a "too many cooks in the kitchen" problem.

Should we shorten a team's sprint cycle during the Dojo?

In a perfect world, yes. Repetition is the name of the game when it comes to skill development, so the more we repeat an entire sprint cycle, the better.

Dion Stewart and Joel Tosi profess two-and-a-half-day sprints in the book *Creating Your Dojo*. I love this approach, in theory. However, in practice, I have not had luck with it because it produces so much anxiety and disturbance that by the time we find a rhythm around two-and-a-half-day sprints, the better part of the Dojo is over.

Instead, I have found a medium with one-week sprints. This gives the team six sprints per Dojo, which still provides a fair amount of repetition and practice, but it doesn't flip their worlds upside down as badly as two-and-a-half-day sprints.

Sometimes the anxiety around altering the sprint cycle can't be overcome, so it is okay to pursue a Dojo following the team's typical sprint cycle. Ultimately, we should be meeting teams where they are at, not shaking things up for the sake of shaking things up.

My advice is to work to get the team on board with one-week sprints when you first meet with them. If it seems like they're a great fit for the Dojo but the one-week sprints are creating a sticking point, conform to their sprint cycle.

What if a Dojo has started but it is not going well for whatever reason?

I was in an in-person Dojo in March 2020 when we were all sent to work from home. After a few days of fumbling with VPNs, Zoom, and blending work and family life for the first time, it was clear that the Dojo could no longer be viable. The team and Dojo coaches unanimously agreed to end the Dojo.

Sometimes Dojos go south for reasons that are not as evident as a worldwide lockdown. It could be low engagement or a slew of unexpected work, but at any point in time, if it appears that the Dojo will not grow the team, then it is time to have a conversation. Perhaps it's with the team. Perhaps it's a conversation with their leadership and a different conversation with the team. In any case, it is important that you discuss the concerns, as it can only result in positive outcomes: (1) the team eagerly tries to get back on track, or (2) the Dojo ends and you are able to engage another team that could draw real benefit from the Dojo.

What do I do if there are no available teams to engage in a Dojo with?

First, find out if this is a short-term or long-term issue.

If it's a short-term issue, take the downtime to work on the Dojo product or pursue professional development for the Dojo coaches. If this is a long-term issue, I've found that it usually comes down to one of three issues. First, it may be time to revisit your Dojo team scoring guide. Is scoring so harsh that it doesn't represent the teams in your organization, causing you to have a small pool of candidate teams?

A second thing to think about is marketing. When was the last time you got the word out about the Dojo? Perhaps it has slipped people's minds, or new people are unaware of it.

Third, has the organization not supported a continuous learning culture? For example, did the organization establish the Dojo practice as a means of upskilling teams but then turn around and inundate teams with so much work and noise that the teams couldn't break away to participate in a Dojo? It may be necessary to get with leadership to discuss how to ensure that teams are available for learning.

How do I manage Dojo administration during a six-week Dojo engagement?

In all honesty, it can be challenging. This is where having multiple Dojo coaches or a person dedicated to Dojo administration shines.

I have been both the lone wolf of a Dojo practice and one of multiple Dojo coaches in a Dojo practice. While you can technically fly solo, having a healthy staff enables better capacity to collaborate and produce better outcomes.

No matter your Dojo staffing, it is wise to establish a cadence to check on your backlog or work related to developing the Dojo product. Heck, you can have the Dojo practice follow Scrum with your very own backlog, standups, plannings, refinements, demos, and retrospectives. Whatever works to drive momentum and accountability.

While in a Dojo, I commit to having at least one session per week to build the Dojo backlog. That is, assessing teams, keeping relationships warm, or putting on a talk to market the Dojo.

Additionally, the coaching intensity becomes low touch around the fourth or fifth week of the Dojo, so I have to leverage the anticipated availability of the Dojo admin.

If I am not in a Dojo, my entire focus is on administration—building the Dojo backlog and enhancing the Dojo product.

What characteristics should I look for when recruiting Dojo coaches?

I have been a Dojo coach at multiple organizations, and I can confidently say that defining, let alone writing, a job description for a Dojo coach can be extremely difficult.

If you examine the traits of a Dojo coach, it sounds like a unicorn.

We're looking for someone who is not only an experienced Agile expert but an experienced technical expert. On top of that, they must be able to navigate meaningful conversations with all levels of the organization (senior leadership to junior developers), sometimes within minutes of each other. What is eyebrow-raising is that this coach has to have a high level of empiricism and confidence that they can enter any situation cold and add value to it.

That description sounds somewhat elitist and gives me a tinge of imposter syndrome as the author of this book. Very few people fit this description, so rather than strictly looking for a unicorn, look for opportunities to develop people as Dojo coaches.

My first Dojo coaching job took a risk with me, as I didn't check every box. Thankfully, they saw the potential and decided to grow me. And look what that became!

To give you something to work with, here are what I consider negotiables and nonnegotiables when recruiting Dojo coach candidates.

NEGOTIABLES
- Doesn't have to be a technical expert—perhaps you have an Agile coach who is out of practice or possesses intermediate technical knowledge; you might be able to upskill them.
- Doesn't have to be an Agile expert—you could have a technical person with proficient Agile knowledge and experience and grow them to become an expert.

NONNEGOTIABLES
- Must have several years of real-world Agile experience.
- Must have several years of real-world technology experience.
- Must be a lifelong learner.
- Must have a high degree of emotional intelligence.

Don't forget to look within your organization for people to develop into Dojo coaches. For instance, technical leads innately have technical experience, usually have Agile and people experience, and may make damn good Dojo coaches.

Can Dojos be shorter than six weeks?

My opinion is no.

Dojos can appear costly if you consider six weeks of a couple of Dojo coaches' time and slowed team performance. So to counter this, some Dojo practices have experimented with hosting two-week Dojos or similarly abridged Dojo engagements. It was a classic case of better throughput.

I was one of those who experimented with hosting a two-week Dojo.

While consulting for a small firm, I helped run a campaign to drum up business by giving away what I called an "appetizer Dojo." It consisted of a complimentary two-week Dojo to demonstrate our Dojo capabilities to a prospective client.

Long story short, I awarded the free Dojo to a phenomenal team that helped run a learning lab themselves.

Despite taking steps to mitigate the risks of shortening a Dojo— limiting the Dojo goals to one and working intensely every day with the team—I still found the two-week Dojo significantly diluted and ineffective in some regions of team development.

Ultimately, the experience was rushed and stressful, adding a heavy cloud of pressure that moved us to complete it like a task instead of treating it as an opportunity to become immersed in learning. In addition, there wasn't any time allotted for digesting the teachings and not enough time to get in good-quality repetitions. There was only time for laser focus on the Dojo goal.

The bottom line is that the two-week Dojo did not provide the time to be human. Did the team learn a new skill in two weeks? Yes. Was it a mildly soul-depleting experience? Unfortunately, yes.

So this won't come as a surprise, but my advice is to keep the engagement to at least six weeks.

As with bourbon, some things shouldn't be rushed because they get better with time.

Can a team go through the Dojo more than once?
Yes!

Though I have extended the length of the Dojo because some engagements benefited from some extra time, I have yet to fulfill my dream of a Dojo sequel.

In theory, you could meaningfully engage in a Dojo with the same team as soon as six months after the initial engagement to work on refining previous or new Dojo goals.

Can a Dojo be done with a nontechnical team?
Yes, absolutely! A Dojo develops long-standing skills through hands-on practice, no matter what those skills may be. The important thing is that you ensure the coaches have the expertise to coach the particular skills featured in said Dojo confidently.

How do I know the Dojo is working?
Are participants *learning* and *retaining* new skills with a smile on their faces? If so, your Dojo is probably working just fine.

Okay, I won't just leave it there. Here is a good list of signs to ensure the Dojo is working for a team.

Signs that a Dojo is working:

- The team is engaged and eager to learn and practice more.
- The team is making steady progress toward their Dojo goals.
- Learning is being retained.
- External parties are starting to notice the team's improvements.
- A growing sense of camaraderie is developing on the team.

How do I know if the Dojo isn't working?
Did you turn your Dojo off and back on again? If only it were that easy!

As in the previous section, here is a list of signs to look for to determine if a Dojo is not working for a team:

- The team is disengaged, quiet, or vapid.
- The team puts little effort into practicing new skills.
- The team members' minds are somewhere else—usually on other work or responsibilities outside the Dojo.

- The team is making no progress toward their Dojo goals.
- The coaches find themselves repeating coaching advice because the team is having a hard time retaining content.

Is the team off-limits during the Dojo engagement?

Yes and no. I'll explain.

While the essence of the Dojo is to intersect learning and delivery so a team can still deliver value to the organization while they learn, the team's performance tends to slow down in the first couple of weeks of the Dojo as they adjust to the engagement. However, midway through the Dojo, the team's performance picks up. It often exceeds the team's previous performance rate because the team can start confidently applying what they have learned from the Dojo. Earlier in the book, I refer to this as "slow down to speed up."

The other aspect to keep in mind is that while the team is still functional in the Dojo, their leadership must give them space for learning. (Note: This is one of the leadership commitments I discussed in the "Intake" section in Chapter 2.) This means leaders should avoid disturbing the Dojo team during the Dojo as much as possible.

So the Dojo team is not off-limits, per se. They are available to deliver, as usual; however, should there be significant changes or fire drills during the Dojo, it will put learning at risk.

Conducting a Dojo is like maintaining a well-tuned car. Can a car run if it misses a few oil changes and tune-ups? Yes, but its performance and longevity suffer if maintenance is neglected. To get the most out of the car, the owner must see maintenance as an investment, not an option.

Why is it called a Dojo?

Dojo is a Japanese term for a room or hall in which judo and other martial arts are practiced. In the dojo, the intent is to offer a space for the hands-on practice of martial arts—often repetitively and deliberately—to develop muscle memory and long-standing habits.

The Agile, product, and tech industries adopted the term *dojo* because they draw inspiration from the hands-on practice approach to achieving long-standing skill-building outcomes.

Dojo also has strong phonetic properties, meaning many find it a neat-sounding buzzword, making it ripe for marketing and exploitation.

The English translation of *dojo* is "place of the way."

Are we culturally appropriating by using the word *dojo*?

In my opinion, yes. I feel that we are unnecessarily borrowing from Japanese culture to describe immersive learning. The use of the word *dojo* was the only factor that made me reluctant to write this book.

But after a ton of soul-searching and discussions with people who are experienced with martial arts dojos, I accepted that the word *dojo* has become a staple in the industry. If I wanted people to find this book and have a shot at becoming stronger immersive learning coaches, I had to concede to using the term.

I dig deeper into this subject, including how to navigate it, in this book's "Cultural Respect" section in the preface.

What requirements does a team need to meet to be Dojo eligible?

As discussed in Chapter 2 in the "Intake" section, you set Dojo eligibility requirements that work best for your organization as a Dojo practice.

For example, I once coached in a Dojo practice that had the condition that a team must be composed of 51 percent or greater full-time employees to be considered for a Dojo.

That said, there are nonnegotiables that I strongly recommend all Dojo practices adhere to.

- Team acceptance of 100 percent—Yes, 100 percent, meaning every single person on the team wants to pursue a Dojo.

If any one team member does not want to pursue a Dojo, the team becomes ineligible for at least that round of Dojos.

- Ready, willing, and available—This means that the team is ready to become engaged in learning, willing to get uncomfortable and do what it takes to learn, and mentally available to receive coaching and free from near-term deadlines that would loom over the Dojo like some type of black cloud.

What should be done if leadership interrupts the Dojo?

Assess and address it immediately because it can jeopardize the value of the Dojo. Leaders set the example, so if the team witnesses their leadership step over the Dojo, they will do the same.

The first thing you'll want to do is assess the interruption. Is it minor or major? Is it a one-time occurrence or a frequent occurrence?

Suppose it's a one-time, minor interruption. In that case, it will probably only take a quick session with leadership to remind them of the importance of the Dojo leadership commitments from the "Intake" section in Chapter 2 with the intent of having the leaders recommit to giving the team space during the Dojo.

An example of a minor, one-time interruption is a fire drill that consumes a couple of hours of the team's attention.

If the interruption seems to be frequent or major—such as multiple war-room-style drills—then I recommend an immediate meeting with leadership to pose a clear ultimatum: no more interruptions or no more Dojo.

Isn't Dojo coaching essentially coaching but timeboxed?

"What makes a Dojo a Dojo?" is a common and valid question often kicked around in the Agile industry and during the intake phase when we're meeting with candidate teams.

On the surface, Dojo coaching can easily be confused with Agile or technical coaching that has been modified with a six-week timebox.

However, several distinguishing factors differentiate Dojo coaching from traditional Agile or technical coaching:

- repetitive practice similar to katas in a martial arts dojo
- going to a different space to learn (physical or virtual Dojo space)
- learning using the team's real work
- full team collaboration and learning
- high-touch, responsive coaching from a skilled expert that produces immediate impact

How do we measure success in the Dojo?

It all comes down to long-standing, transformative skill, habit, and behavior development. No matter the Dojo or Dojo goals, that's the epitome of success in the Dojo.

Throughout the Dojo, there will be exciting breakthroughs that occur that help fuel momentum for long-term, retentive growth. We will refer to Dojo metrics to monitor the progress of the team. But it is not until the 90-day check-in that we know if success was achieved for a particular Dojo.

After 90 days, the team will have practiced what was taught by the Dojo coaches on their own for 3 months. At that time, whatever detractors that would have come into the picture to induce bad habits or hinder good practices would have presented themselves.

The 90-day test is the ultimate validation of sustainability and genuine, transformative growth.

Supporting materials for this book can be found at
dojopocketguide.com

Bibliography

Adkins, Lyssa. *Coaching Agile Teams: A Companion for ScrumMasters, Agile Coaches, and Project Managers in Transition*. Upper Saddle River, NJ: Addison-Wesley, 2010.

Amazon. *2021 Annual Report*. Accessed October 4, 2022. https://s2.q4cdn.com/299287126/files/doc_financials/2022/ar/Amazon-2021-Annual-Report.pdf.

Apple. Form 10-K for fiscal year 2021. US Securities and Exchange Commission. Accessed October 4, 2022. https://s2.q4cdn.com/470004039/files/doc_financials/2021/q4/_10-K-2021-%28As-Filed%29.pdf.

Ashford, Susan, and James R. Detert. "Get the Boss to Buy In." *Harvard Business Review*, January–February 2015. https://hbr.org/2015/01/get-the-boss-to-buy-in.

Bache, Emily. *Technical Agile Coaching with the Samman Method*. Leanpub, 2021.

Beck, Kent. *Extreme Programming*. Paris: CampusPress, 2002.

Bowman, Sharon L. *Training from the Back of the Room! 65 Ways to Step Aside and Let Them Learn*. San Francisco: Jossey-Bass, 2009.

Clacey, Kirsten, and Jay-Allen Morris. *The Remote Facilitator's Pocket Guide*. Oakland, CA: Berrett-Koehler, 2020.

Coyle, Daniel. *The Culture Code: The Secrets of Highly Successful Groups*. London: Random House, 2019.

Duignan, Brian. "Dunning-Kruger Effect." *Encyclopædia Britannica*. Accessed June 1, 2022. https://www.britannica.com/science/Dunning-Kruger-effect.

Gillibrand, Kirsten. "Reforming the Way Washington Works." *Huffpost*, July 20, 2010.

Gothelf, Jeff, and Josh Seiden. *Lean UX: Creating Great Products with Agile Teams*. Sebastopol, CA: O'Reilly Media, 2021.

Knight, Rebecca. "McKinsey Knows Why Your Employees Are Quitting—and It's Not about the Money." Business Insider, September 8, 2021. https://www .businessinsider.com/mckinsey-employees-feeling-undervalued-at-work-2021-9.

Leffingwell, Dean. "Continuous Learning Culture." Scaled Agile Framework, September 27, 2021. https://www.scaledagileframework.com/continuous-learning -culture/.

Lindenfors, Patrik, Andreas Wartel, and Johan Lind. "'Dunbar's Number' Deconstructed." *Biology Letters* 17, no. 5 (2021). https://doi.org/10.1098/rsbl.2021.0158.

McCandless, Keith, and Henri Lipmanowicz. "Making Space with TRIZ." Liberating Structures. Accessed June 1, 2022. https://www.liberatingstructures.com /6-making-space-with-triz/.

———. "1-2-4-All." Liberating Structures. Accessed June 1, 2022. https://www .liberatingstructures.com/1-1-2-4-all/.

McFeely, Shane, and Ben Wigert. "This Fixable Problem Costs U.S. Businesses $1 Trillion." Gallup, March 13, 2019. https://www.gallup.com/workplace/247391 /fixable-problem-costs-businesses-trillion.aspx#:~:text=The%20cost%20of%20 replacing%20an,to%20%242.6%20million%20per%20year.

Medina, John. *Brain Rules: 12 Principles for Surviving and Thriving at Work, Home, and School*. Seattle: Pear Press, 2014.

Merriam-Webster. "Dictionary by Merriam-Webster: America's Most-Trusted Online Dictionary." Accessed September 15, 2022. https://www.merriam-webster .com/.

Netflix. Form 10-K for fiscal year 2021. Accessed October 4, 2022. https://s22.q4cdn .com/959853165/files/doc_financials/2021/q4/da27d24b-9358-4b5c-a424-6da061d9 1836.pdf.

Pease, Allan, and Barbara Pease. *The Definitive Book of Body Language*. Batu Caves, Selangor, Malaysia: PTS Publishing House, 2018.

Perna, Mark C. "Why Skill and Career Advancement Are the Way to Gen-Z's Heart." *Forbes*, March 2, 2021. https://www.forbes.com/sites/markcperna/2021/03 /02/why-skill-and-career-advancement-are-the-way-to-gen-zs-heart/?sh=2ce74de 022b5.

Pichler, Roman. "The Product Vision Board." Roman Pichler's website, December 17, 2021. https://www.romanpichler.com/tools/product-vision-board/.

Pink, Daniel H. *Drive: The Surprising Truth about What Motivates Us*. New York: Riverhead Books, 2013.

Pontefract, Dan. "The Wasted Dollars of Corporate Training Programs." *Forbes*, September 15, 2019. https://www.forbes.com/sites/danpontefract/2019/09/15/the -wasted-dollars-of-corporate-training-programs/?sh=4b41c4b971f9.

Pope, Verl T., and Christopher Lawrence. "Virginia Satir Model." In *The SAGE Encyclopedia of Marriage, Family, and Couples Counseling*, edited by Jon Carlson and Shannon B. Dermer, 4:1753–1758. Thousand Oaks, CA: SAGE, 2017. https://doi.org /10.4135/9781483369532.n525.

Priestley, Daniel. *Oversubscribed: How to Get People Lining Up to Do Business with You*. Chichester, UK: Wiley, 2020.

Rusmanica, Tudor. "How to Create More Shareable Content in 7 Steps." Bigwave Marketing, May 25, 2021. https://bigwave.co.uk/blog/the-7-step-process-for-more -shareable-content/.

Schafer, Jack. *The Like Switch: An Ex-FBI Agent's Guide to Influencing, Attracting, and Winning People Over*. With Marvin Karlins. New York: Atria Paperback, 2019.

Scott, Kim. *Radical Candor: Be a Kick-Ass Boss without Losing Your Humanity*. New York: St. Martin's, 2019.

Smart, Jonathan. *Sooner Safer Happier: Antipatterns and Patterns for Business Agility*. Portland, OR: IT Revolution, 2021.

Statista Research Department. "Average Spend on Workplace Training per Employee Worldwide from 2008 to 2020 (in U.S. Dollars)." Statista, December 2021. https://www.statista.com/statistics/738519/workplace-training-spending -per-employee/#:~:text=The%20average%20per%2Demployee%20spending,worker %20on%20learning%20and%20development.

Stewart, Dion, and Joel Tosi. *Creating Your Dojo: Upskill Your Organization for Digital Evolution*. Austin, TX: Lioncrest, 2019.

Target. "The Target Dojo." Accessed June 1, 2022. https://dojo.target.com/.

Wagner, Robert W. "Edgar Dale: Professional." *Theory into Practice* 9, no. 2 (1970): 89–95. https://doi.org/10.1080/00405847009542259.

Whitler, Kimberly A. "3 Reasons Why Storytelling Should Be a Priority for Marketers." *Forbes*, July 16, 2018. https://www.forbes.com/sites/kimberlywhitler /2018/07/14/3-reasons-why-storytelling-should-be-a-priority-for-marketers/?sh =301a5a476758.

Whitworth, Laura. *Co-active Coaching: New Skills for Coaching People toward Success in Work and Life*. Boston: Davies-Black, 2009.

Acknowledgments

To Berrett-Koehler for giving me, a first-time author, an opportunity to publish a book.

To the Dojo community for their support, feedback, and inspiration.

To field experts Alex Basa, Emily Koehler, and Lisa Turnbull for reviewing this book and providing feedback that genuinely enhanced the overall quality.

To Lisa Turnbull for the support (emotional and comedic) to complete this book.

To the ACE Team for showing me the place of the way.

To Gryffindog and Doniphan for being the cutest and cuddliest office mates.

Note: Page numbers followed by *f* or *t* indicate a figure or table on the designated page

About the Author

Longtime agilist Jess Brock was introduced to the Dojo in 2019. Intrigued by a Dojo coaching role description that emphasized growing others more than driving delivery, Jess applied for the role with no prior knowledge of immersive learning Dojos. She got the job, but never dreamed it would be career defining.

Soon into her Dojo coaching journey, it was evident that she connected deeply with the intent, value, and spirit of the Dojo. Perhaps it can be attributed to her "Show Me State" Missouri roots that Jess fell in love with the "less theory, more doing" approach to coaching.

The Dojo inspires Jess in many ways, and she has given back to the Dojo community through her talks, blogs, and now this book.

As of 2023, Jess has led dozens of Dojo engagements, spanning three countries and physical and virtual settings.

Dear reader,

Thank you for picking up this book and welcome to the worldwide BK community! You're joining a special group of people who have come together to create positive change in their lives, organizations, and communities.

What's BK all about?

Our mission is to connect people and ideas to create a world that works for all.

Why? Our communities, organizations, and lives get bogged down by old paradigms of self-interest, exclusion, hierarchy, and privilege. But we believe that can change. That's why we seek the leading experts on these challenges—and share their actionable ideas with you.

A welcome gift

To help you get started, we'd like to offer you a **free copy** of one of our bestselling ebooks:

www.bkconnection.com/welcome

When you claim your **free ebook**, you'll also be subscribed to our blog.

Our freshest insights

Access the best new tools and ideas for leaders at all levels on our blog at ideas.bkconnection.com.

Sincerely,

Your friends at Berrett-Koehler

Certified

Corporation